About This Book

Why is this topic important?

Companies have spent millions of dollars on initiatives to increase the number people of color (POC) they employ. Yet, many have watched their multimillion dollar investments disappear as these talented POC leave their organizations at an alarming rate. To answer the question of "why," leaders and managers have turned to surveys, focus groups, and interviews to identify the reasons for these departures. They have developed numerous strategies and programs to reduce the turnover. However, the results of these retention strategies have been disappointing, and POC continue to leave organizations. In this book we identify the key issue contributing to the continuous departure of POC: *There is often a vast difference between the way POC view the organizations in which they work and the way that leaders and managers view these same organizations.*

As organizations attempt to reverse this negative trend and make sustainable change in increasing the representation of POC in their workforces, it will become increasingly important to understand the real issues that motivate POC to leave. Companies that fail to examine and understand the root cause for the departure of POC will continue to experience this revolving door—where POC come in the organization's door, and go back out in a short period of time.

What can you achieve with this book?

This book uses a fable, based on actual corporate situations, to help leaders and managers understand not only what it takes to recruit, but also what it takes to retain people of color in a highly competitive marketplace. Additionally, the book contains assessments to assist the reader in identifying personal behaviors as well as organizational conditions that contribute to the turnover of POC. This book is designed to help leaders and managers:

1. Understand that POC often have different experiences in the organization, and thus different views from their own.

2. Look beyond the obvious blunders to the behavioral subtleties and nuances that impact retention among POC.

3. Practice identifying and addressing the real issues that prompt POC to leave organizations.

4. Use the practical tools in the book to guide their interactions with POC in the organization, enhancing their ability to retain them.

How is this book organized?

This book is designed as a simple, practical, hands-on resource guide for retaining POC. A mirror comes to life throughout the book and prompts leaders and managers to look at organizational situations from a broad perspective, not just their own, and answer this question from the point of view of POC, *Do You See What I See?*

Chapter 1 describes the challenge of retaining people of color in organizations. Chapter 2 brings the issue to life using a corporate fable, "A Tale of Lessons Learned Corporation (LLC)." After the fable is told, readers are invited to analyze what went wrong as LLC attempted, and subsequently failed, to build a pool of talented POC.

Chapter 3 provides the reader the opportunity to examine each of the major events in the fable, and consider the different views held by leaders, managers, and POC.

Chapter 4 introduces a four-step retention model to help organizations retain POC. This model establishes "valuing" as the foundation for retaining POC in organizations. Additionally, it identifies the behaviors in which leaders and managers must engage—from recruitment through the duration of their tenure—to demonstrate that they "value" POC. In this chapter readers are invited to take critical assessments to help them determine whether their behaviors promote the retention or the departure of POC.

Chapter 5 provides an opportunity for leaders and managers to practice their skill in "valuing" and retaining POC through ten scenarios. These common organizational scenarios offer the reader the opportunity to (a) select a course of action from a list of four responses, (b) examine how POC may view this course of action, and (c) consider the impact this choice may have on the retention of POC.

Chapter 6 concludes with an extensive list of practical tools and behaviors that the reader may use to support and interact with POC more effectively, and enhance the company's ability to retain them.

About Pfeiffer

Pfeiffer serves the professional development and hands-on resource needs of training and human resource practitioners and gives them products to do their jobs better. We deliver proven ideas and solutions from experts in HR development and HR management, and we offer effective and customizable tools to improve workplace performance. From novice to seasoned professional, Pfeiffer is the source you can trust to make yourself and your organization more successful.

Essential Knowledge Pfeiffer produces insightful, practical, and comprehensive materials on topics that matter the most to training and HR professionals. Our Essential Knowledge resources translate the expertise of seasoned professionals into practical, how-to guidance on critical workplace issues and problems. These resources are supported by case studies, worksheets, and job aids and are frequently supplemented with CD-ROMs, websites, and other means of making the content easier to read, understand, and use.

Essential Tools Pfeiffer's Essential Tools resources save time and expense by offering proven, ready-to-use materials—including exercises, activities, games, instruments, and assessments—for use during a training or team-learning event. These resources are frequently offered in looseleaf or CD-ROM format to facilitate copying and customization of the material.

Pfeiffer also recognizes the remarkable power of new technologies in expanding the reach and effectiveness of training. While e-hype has often created whizbang solutions in search of a problem, we are dedicated to bringing convenience and enhancements to proven training solutions. All our e-tools comply with rigorous functionality standards. The most appropriate technology wrapped around essential content yields the perfect solution for today's on-the-go trainers and human resource professionals.

Pfeiffer *Essential resources for training and HR professionals*
www.pfeiffer.com

Do You See What I See?

A Diversity Tale for Retaining People of Color

Janice Fenn
Chandra Goforth Irvin

Pfeiffer
A Wiley Imprint
www.pfeiffer.com

Published by Pfeiffer
An Imprint of Wiley
989 Market Street, San Francisco, CA 94103-1741 www.pfeiffer.com

Readers should be aware that Internet websites offered as citations and/or sources for further information may have changed or disappeared between the time this was written and when it is read.

For additional copies/bulk purchases of this book in the U.S. please contact 800-274-4434.

Pfeiffer books and products are available through most bookstores. To contact Pfeiffer directly call our Customer Care Department within the U.S. at 800-274-4434, outside the U.S. at 317-572-3985, fax 317-572-4002, or visit www.pfeiffer.com.

Pfeiffer also publishes its books in a variety of electronic formats. Some content that appears in print may not be available in electronic books.

Library of Congress Cataloging-in-Publication Data
Fenn, Janice.
Do you see what I see?: a diversity tale for retaining people of color / Janice Fenn, Chandra Goforth Irvin.
    p. cm.
Includes index.
    ISBN-10 0-7879-7878-7 (alk. paper)
    ISBN-13 978-0-7879-7878-5 (alk. paper)
  1. Diversity in the workplace. 2. Employee retention. I. Irvin, Chandra Goforth, 1956- II. Title.
    HF5549.5.M5F46 2005
    658.300'8—dc22

2005002450

Acquiring Editor: Lisa Shannon

Director of Development: Kathleen Dolan Davies

Developmental Editor: Susan Rachmeler

Production Editor: Dawn Kilgore

Editor: Rebecca Taff

Manufacturing Supervisor: Becky Carreño

Editorial Assistant: Laura Reizman

Interior Design: Suzanne Albertson

Printed in the United States of America
Printing 10 9 8 7 6 5 4 3 2 1

CONTENTS

ACKNOWLEDGMENTS

We'd like to express our sincere appreciation to Dr. Price Cobbs for his guidance, mentoring support and insightful and candid feedback on the manuscript. We are grateful to Jackie and Floyd Dickens for their coaching, candor, and that single comment that inspired us to reorganize the book. A special thank you to Gary Johnson for introducing us to Jackie and Floyd. Many thanks to Stan Davis, Chere Nabor and Gerry Fernandez for reviewing the manuscript. Your feedback came at a time when we really, really needed it. We deeply appreciate the human resources, organizational development, and diversity professionals from twenty-one corporations who committed to preordering copies of this book, giving us an incredible vote of confidence. We extend our thanks to Beth Hopkins for editorial assistance, and Brent Ohlmann for legal guidance and infinite patience. To our editors at Pfeiffer—Lisa Shannon, Kathleen Dolan Davies, and Dawn Kilgore— we offer a hardy "thank you" for your support and flexibility. Most importantly, we are tremendously grateful to our extended families whose love sustains us, and who have continued to ask, "Is the book ready yet?" Well finally, the book is ready!

INTRODUCTION

It was all that she could do to contain herself. Finally, after all these years, she, the school's ugly duckling, the girl who hardly ever had a date, the one who was shy and afraid and virtually unknown among her peers, was returning to her high school class reunion as a star!

She had dreamed of making a grand entrance into an auditorium filled with classmates who knew of her great success. They would whisper in awe among themselves as she slowly made her way to the microphone to perform a few tunes from her latest hit album.

As she touched up her makeup in the bathroom mirror, she prayed that she would be humble as she performed for her classmates. Then, with one last glimpse in the mirror, she dashed off to the auditorium.

It was just as she had dreamed. As she slowly and gracefully made her way toward the stage, the murmur of the crowd grew louder and louder, confirming in her mind that she had indeed "arrived." Although she had prayed for humility, she could barely contain her pride. "How wonderful it is to be here," she thought. But her pride turned to horror as she realized that the buzz of the crowd was not the sound of adoration or respect, but the sound of surprise, embarrassment, and mirth. For the crowd had seen something she had not seen—the hem of her dress tucked into the back of her pantyhose!

We do not know who the woman was, but we immediately drew the parallel with managers and organization leaders when we heard her story. Just as this woman misinterpreted the cause for the stir of the crowd, managers and organization leaders often misjudge the cause for the stir of discontentment from people of color (POC).

In this scenario, the woman imagined that what others were viewing was her stately entrance into the auditorium. Because she did not see the hem of her dress tucked into the back of her pantyhose—exposing an unflattering view—it never occurred to her that the crowd was seeing something different or that there was anything else to see. It is easy to understand why she believed the murmur of the crowed was a result of adulation and awe.

A similar scenario plays out in many organizations that are experiencing high turnover among people of color. Managers and leaders receive feedback regarding the status of people of color in the organization or regarding those who are leaving the organization. Yet, since these leaders and managers view the organization through their own experiences, they misinterpret this feedback. In this case, the woman's limited perspective prevented her from seeing what the audience saw. In organizations, often the limited perspective of leaders and managers prevents them from seeing what people of color see regarding the organizational realities.

This does not mean that leaders do not want to see the picture from the view of people of color. The young woman in this story took a last glimpse in the mirror and entered the auditorium. What she imagined the audience saw is what she had just seen in the mirror. It never occurred to her that the crowd was fixated on her exposed posterior. The woman viewed only her face in the mirror. The result is that she missed critically important details. Leaders and managers view their organizations as well, through opinion surveys, focus groups, and interviews. However, they too consider only the face value and miss vital information. Often it is this very information that they overlook that leads to the departure of POC.

In the course of our consulting practices, we have found that this is the case in many organizations that are losing talented POC at an alarming rate. There is a vast difference between the way POC view the organizations in which they work and the way managers and leaders see these same organizations.

When managers are asked to explain their poor retention of POC, there is a tendency for the leaders and executives of these companies to accept one-sided rationales—those of the managers—that discount the negative organizational experiences of POC. Executives permit excuses and justifications from managers who have failed to develop these individuals. They allow themselves to be convinced that they cannot change the negative impact that the organizational culture may have on POC. In other words, they accept explanations for POCs' departure that absolve their organizations of any accountability.

In this book, we identify and discuss discrepancies between the views of managers and views of POC they manage using a fable of an organization, its leaders, managers, and newly recruited POC. In this fable, a mirror comes to life and offers different views to help executives and managers understand not only what it takes to recruit, but what it takes to *retain* POC in a highly competitive marketplace. Moreover, through this fable you will be able to examine step by step what happened, what should have happened, conclusions that were drawn, and conclusions that should have been drawn. Using the example of the organization in our fable, you will have the opportunity to practice identifying and addressing the real issues that result in people of color leaving organizations.

WHY THE MIRRORS?

Throughout the book we use a mirror as the metaphor to provide feedback and insight into diversity issues. We chose a mirror as a symbol of what companies must use in order to examine the root cause of why POC leave organizations and what the organization can use to prevent their departure. Holding up a mirror can allow you to see what is really there. However, an organization must *choose to look*! If organization leaders make a conscious decision to stand in front of a mirror, they will be able to see and take in an abundance of information regarding the experiences of POC.

However, in order for this to work, they must *select a good mirror*. It is critical to use a reflection tool that has great clarity and is undistorted in any way. The mirror should not be marred, smudged, cracked, or curved, nor should there be any glare or other obstructions on the surface to block the view.

Moreover, organization leaders must select a mirror that provides *a reflection from many angles.* The frontal view should be only a first step. Reflections will be needed from side angles, rear angles, and top and bottom angles. There should be frequent use of three-way mirrors to provide views from many angles simultaneously. Such a complete view will reflect the realities within the organization. Then, and only then, will organizational leaders begin to understand the real reasons why they are losing their POC talent.

In this book the mirror will be used to help managers and leaders: (1) understand that people of color may have a view of the organization that is different from their own; (2) acknowledge and examine the subtle differences and nuances in managerial interactions with POC that lead POC to view the organization differently than their managers; (3) examine these different views and the resulting conclusions that lead to the departure of POC and the perplexity and confusion on the part of the organization; and (4) identify practical tools and solutions that can be used to retain people of color. With these insights and tools, leaders and managers can begin the process of helping their organizations increase their retention levels.

THE INTRODUCTION OF DIVERSITY INITIATIVES IN ORGANIZATIONS

The initial objective for introducing diversity initiatives in organizations was to increase the numbers of women and POC (individuals from ethnic backgrounds such as African Americans, Hispanics, Asians, and Native Americans). Led by a few pioneer companies such as IBM and Xerox, this trend gained even more momentum in 1988 when the Hudson Institute released its landmark *Workforce 2000* report. An applied research organization that focuses on future trends, the Hudson Institute reported the startling news that by 2000 the majority of the net new entrants to the workforce would be women, people of color, and immigrants. The result was that a large number of companies quickly launched diversity initiatives aimed at increasing the numbers of women and people of color, in an effort to position themselves as an employer of choice for the future.

Critics of these corporate diversity initiatives argued that diversity encompassed a broad range of differences that employees brought to the workplace. Since most companies' diversity initiatives were focused on increasing the numbers of women and POC, they were really nothing more than sophisticated affirmative action goals. In response, corporate proponents of diversity readily acknowledged that diversity included more than race and gender, but remained steadfast in their focus on increasing the numbers of women and people of color.

Marilyn Loden, a nationally recognized organizational change consultant, developed a model, The Diversity Wheel, which served as an important tool and resource to explain why organizations initially identified select aspects of diversity as their focus. In her model Loden pointed out that diversity includes *primary characteristics* such as race, gender, age, ethnicity, physical ability, and sexual orientation, differences that are visible, non-changeable, and innate, for the most part. Additionally, Loden showed that diversity includes a myriad of *secondary characteristics* such as marital status, income, religion, military status, parental status, and occupation. The list of secondary charactistics, which could continue indefinitely, includes non-physical characteristics that are not necessarily visible to others and are changeable, for the most part.

While all diverse characteristics are important to consider, certain differences—the *primary diversity characteristics*—have a greater impact on individual opportunities. In most cases, it is because these differences are in fact so visible. Yet individuals have no choice over visible differences because they are part of the package in which they are born.

According to Janet Elsea, in the book *The Four Minute Sell,* when we come in contact with other individuals, what we notice first are skin color, gender, and age—in that order. Even in organizations, one of the first things that we observe is the physical make-up (*primary characteristics*) of the workforce: the numbers of people of color, women, and individuals in various age categories. As organizations began to consider how they were viewed by this demographically different workforce, they correctly ascertained that it would be difficult to convince their employees, outside observers, and corporate America at large that they were valuing diversity if these more visible aspects of diversity (*primary characteristics*) were not evident.

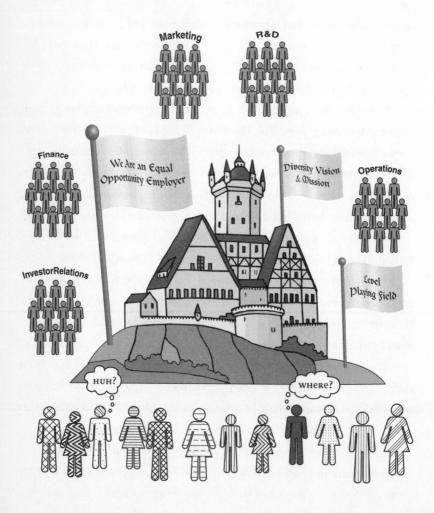

As a result, some companies adopted a master plan with an initial focus on increasing the *visible* diversity in their organizations. Their intent was to value and leverage the visible diversity, after which they would focus on the non-visible aspects of diversity such as diverse thought, perspectives, approaches, religion, geographic origins, and so forth. Focusing on the visible diversity characteristics first seemed not only a reasonable approach, but a strategic one; and subsequently other organizations embraced this same strategy.

ACTIONS COMPANIES HAVE TAKEN

Organizations have spent millions of dollars to increase the number of women and POC they employ. They have engaged internal and external advisors. They have revamped diversity programs to include accountability measures. They have offered diversity awareness and skills training to leaders, managers, and employees. Some have launched diversity awards programs and integrated diversity into their public relations, vendor, and communications programs.

Additionally, many companies have conducted organizational assessments, turnover studies, and demographic studies, the results of which have motivated these organizations to expand their concept of what is required to retain diverse talent. For instance, a company that was once satisfied with affirmative action goals may now tie executive bonuses to development of women and POC. Table I.1 illustrates the extent to which organizations have worked to increase their diversity.

Although complex and comprehensive, the question is, "Have these efforts worked?" To some extent they have. The initiatives are sound, and organizations that have used them have been largely successful in attracting outstanding, diverse talent from all groups. Nonetheless, after more than a decade of devoting incredible resources to attracting and hiring women and POC and experiencing success in hiring both of these groups, many organizations have failed to increase their overall representation of

- Assessments
- Turnover studies
- Shared vision
- Retention objectives
- Performance measurements
- Management accountability
- POC and female representation at all levels and on board of directors
- Targeted online recruiting
- Target search firm's work
- Search firm bonuses/penalties
- Exemplary employee models
- Career fairs
- Scholarships for POC and females
- University partnerships
- Pre-employment reality visits
- Substantive student internships
- Work/life programs
- Sabbaticals
- Business exchange programs
- "Stretch" projects/assignments
- Accelerated learning
- Cross-functional training
- Promotions and advancements

- Competitive pay
- Pay equity
- Sign-on bonuses
- "Stay" bonuses
- Performance bonuses
- Daily chats with new employees
- Special trips and perks
- Cross-cultural festivals and events
- Cross-cultural dialogues
- Book reviews, speakers, videos
- Affinity groups
- Affinity group exchanges
- Affinity groups as business resources
- Tuition reimbursements
- Redeployment
- Mentoring
- Coaching
- Buddy programs
- Sponsorships targeted at POC and women
- Internal company awards
- External awards ("best place to work...")
- Community advisory councils

Table I.1. Examples of Diversity Strategies
From the Professional Resources Organization, Inc., and Irvin, Goforth & Irvin, LLC, consulting experiences.

women and POC. In fact, some companies appear to have a revolving door where women and POC are concerned, quickly losing the talent that they've just recruited.

NARROWING THE FOCUS

Organizations are puzzled, challenged, and alarmed by their inability to retain women and people of color, especially after exhaustive efforts to attract and hire them. Of these two demographic groups, retention of POC has become more problematic. This issue has been the focus of numerous studies, discussion groups, consultations, articles, and presentations.

For this reason we are devoting this book to addressing only *one* aspect of diversity, *retaining POC*. We wholeheartedly acknowledge the broad range of diversity issues, the fact that organizations may not have met their gender goals either, and the complexity of other primary characteristics of diversity such as age and sexual orientation. Yet, retaining POC is an issue that has paralyzed many corporate diversity initiatives and continues to be the Achilles heel for these companies.

Why All the Fuss Over Retaining People of Color?

Organizations take the issue of retention of all employees seriously because of the high costs associated with turnover. Consider the *direct* impact of recruiting alone, including advertising, travel expenses, sign-on incentives, relocation, orientation, training, and sometimes the cost of temporary employees to fill in critical functions. In addition, there may even be significant search firm fees. The *indirect* costs include the time that recruiters and other executives spend sourcing, qualifying, and interviewing talent. Companies attempting to quantify and track this cost use a variety of formulas to calculate the dollar value of retention. Ernst & Young, a prominent accounting firm, calculates conservatively that the cost of turnover may be as much as four times an employee's annual salary. The ability to retain POC is an even greater issue for organizations, since the attrition rate for POC is often higher.

What Accounts for High Turnover Rates Among POC?

Certainly, shifts in workforce demographics and other related issues often contribute to escalating turnover rates. However, post-exit interviews reveal that other key factors accelerate and often prompt the exodus of POC.

The tale that follows describes a situation that leaders and managers in organizations often encounter. It chronicles how a corporation developed a strategy to hire POC, executed the strategy successfully, yet lost these people of color in the end. The fable demonstrates how, even with the best intentions, organizations can miss critical signals that, if addressed, would allow them to retain talented POC.

CHAPTER 1

The Tale

Mirror, Mirror on the Wall,
Are We Doomed to Lose Them All?
A Too Familiar Tale of Recruitment and Retention

ONCE UPON A TIME IN THE MYTHICAL LAND of Corporate America, there existed a financially successful corporation whose divisions, workers, and products were spread around the world. This mythical corporation was called Lessons Learned Corporation, Inc. (LLC).

LLC heard about the workforce 2000 statistics announced by the Hudson Institute and decided that it would position itself strategically to meet the demands of a changing marketplace and workforce, whose new entrants would be primarily women, POC, and immigrants. In order to respond to marketplace demands created by these changing demographics, this particular company decided to launch a plan to recruit the best POC in the country from the top MBA schools. All executives were charged with helping the company achieve this goal.

One of the current MBAs, Carrie DeLoad, was assigned to organize this comprehensive recruiting effort. Carrie was charged with ensuring that the proper relationships were forged and contacts made to facilitate this initiative.

Carrie DeLoad organized recruiting events for the corporation across the country. There were presentations, receptions, and luncheons hosted by top company executives; scholarships, awards, special events for on-campus minority clubs; gifts of company product; private invitations to interview from company executives; campus mailings; and newspaper ads. All were designed to attract a larger than normal turnout of POC.

With the promise of challenging and high-visibility assignments, high salaries, sign-on bonuses, relocation, and other perks, the potential for cross-training, and top executive positions within ten years, LLC was successful in hiring forty MBAs of color, 40 percent of the one hundred MBAs the company hired over a two-year period.

The following is the profile of these MBAs who were POC: top MBA schools, top rankings of their classes, and previous corporate experiences. They were corporately polished. THEY HAD CREDENTIALS! The company was incredibly excited and reported their numbers far and wide throughout the land of Corporate America. Of course, Carrie DeLoad was pleased with such wonderful results.

A few months later a cry came out of the land that some of the new hires were not happy. Some of the recently hired POC MBAs were claiming that they had been given mediocre assignments. Others were not treated well by their managers. In many cases they were the last to be promoted in their peer group of new hires. Additionally, they were not being given recognition for a job well done. Some were even thinking of leaving and called to inform Carrie DeLoad.

Having heard the news, Carrie immediately contacted the division executives where these MBAs were working. The executives were in disbelief! How could this be? They had not heard anything of the sort, but they would investigate. The executives sought out the POC MBAs to discuss the situation, and the POC gave examples of the disparate treatment they had endured from their managers.

The executives shared these examples with the managers of these POC, who disclaimed and disavowed any knowledge of disparate treatment. In fact, the managers were indignant and appalled that such claims could be alleged. However, in the face of evidence, they did admit that some POC had been promoted last and/or had not been placed in the high-visibility assignments. Nonetheless, there was a reasonable explanation for these acts. These POC needed more seasoning, and they needed to learn to operate more strategically. "Did you want us to promote them before they were ready?" they asked.

Equipped with the managers' explanations, the executives reported back to Ms. DeLoad and to the executive team at LLC that there were a few bumps in the road, but all was well. Besides, they argued, "White males were unhappy with some of their assignments too, and the company should not place an inordinate focus on any one group."

Mirror, mirror, the recruits are disgusted.
They say their managers cannot be trusted.

If the managers say they're
doing their best,
Here's what I suggest.
Communicate a new cultural norm.
Then challenge your managers
to conform.

However, the bits and pieces of information that some POC shared directly with Carrie DeLoad were inconsistent with the explanations that their managers had provided. So Ms. DeLoad suggested that formal feedback sessions be conducted. During the feedback sessions, POC were cautious but forthcoming enough to share some experiences and scenarios that concerned the company. Acknowledging potential problems with how the POC had been treated, the company admonished its division executives to correct and monitor these situations.

Again, for a short time it appeared that all was well. Then one by one, POC MBAs with some of the finest credentials began to leave LLC. During exit interviews, these MBAs gave the following reasons to the company for their departure: (1) they wanted to join the family business; (2) they were leaving because a spouse or significant other was elsewhere; (3) the city where they were working just did not provide enough cultural enrichment; and (4) another company contacted them and made an offer that they could not refuse. Since the reasons that the POC offered for their departure were reasonable, the LLC management never thought to probe for further information.

Nevertheless, executives wanted to prevent more POC exits from happening. When asked about preventative measures, Carrie DeLoad suggested that LLC hire an outside consulting firm to conduct post-exit interviews. The goal would be to get in-depth information on the reasons for the departures of POC. "What a great idea!" said the company executives.

The feedback that the people of color provided to the consulting firm was startlingly different from the feedback these same people of color had provided to LLC upon departure. Had these MBAs been untruthful in their conversations with LLC? No, but they had been evasive. The consulting firm indicated that the people of color simply had not told the entire truth in order to preserve relationships and avoid burning bridges.

Yes, they may have joined the family business, but it was because they were disillusioned over their reception, treatment, and assignments at LLC. They may have relocated to be with a significant other or spouse, but it was because of their frustration with their current situation that they even considered the move. The city where they were working may not have been a cultural Mecca, but they were building networks and finding ways to enrich their personal lives. Yes, a recruiter or a company may have contacted them, but they would never have considered the offer had they been happy with their current assignments.

They had come to LLC committed to building a future. They had left shortly thereafter, disillusioned and disappointed by the lack of response from executives to whom they had communicated their plight.

The final report issued by the consulting firm confirmed the real reasons for the departures. The POC expressed the following reactions:

1. They were disheartened by their managers' personal reactions to them: giving them mediocre assignments, not valuing or rewarding their contributions, and promoting them last out of all their peers, even after outstanding performance. They discovered some managers had a history of this type of behavior with more than one person of color.
2. They were upset that the promise of developmental assignments, opportunities for cross-functional training, and true mentors never materialized for them.
3. They knew that once they pointed out the above issues, they would be labeled as complainers. Furthermore, they felt that, with this label, they would not be successful in the future.

When the company gave the managers the specific feedback, the managers explained, "These individuals were not as sharp as we first believed. They just were not meeting performance expectations. Besides, we think that they are overly sensitive and prone to emotional over-reaction."

The company leaders accepted these explanations and proceeded with business as usual, feeling that they had ultimately weeded out the hiring mistakes that any company is prone to make. Meanwhile, the feedback from POC continued, the rationales and excuses prevailed, and the exodus persisted until all but a few POC were gone.

Follow-up studies indicated that POC had landed positions with Fortune 100 companies, at higher levels, and with higher pay. The same POC who had departed LLC had taken their chest of credentials and skills, moved elsewhere, and been successful.

There was much wringing of hands and gnashing of teeth as LLC wondered, "What happened? How could such good intentions go awry? How could we have selected so many people who were inappropriate for their roles?"

In a brief moment of introspection, some asked whether there was any merit to the allegations of disparate treatment. Alas, the answer from many of those who had been accused was, "No, we didn't do anything wrong. Turnover is a fact of corporate life."

Nonetheless, LLC was not accustomed to defeat and decided that it would try again. This time, however, LLC vowed to be more strategic. They would allow other companies to bear the cost of the on-campus MBA recruiting. LLC would take its POC talent from other companies throughout the mythical land of Corporate America.

They were successful in the second recruiting effort, hiring a significant number of highly skilled POC from other organizations. Determined to retain them this time, LLC held conferences to allow POC to meet top LLC executives. They formed a task force of POC whose purpose was to recruit and retain other POC. They set goals for the development of POC.

To their dismay, history began to repeat itself. Complaints about mediocre assignments, biased treatment by managers, and lack of promotions resurfaced—and so did the exodus! One by one POC left LLC, and each gave one of the following reasons for his or her departure: (1) it was an offer that I just could not refuse; (2) I am relocating to be near a spouse or significant other; and (3) the location just is not culturally nurturing.

An uproar swept through the corporation. Division executives were asked to explain what happened, and reports on POC attrition were provided for each location. Managers with responsibility for POC made

presentations to executive committees. Finally, the company acknowl-edged that the environment was not nurturing for POC. Nevertheless, there were no repercussions for any of the managers involved.

LLC's management was discouraged, but it accepted that this was "just not meant to be." Times had changed, and LLC could not launch another massive recruiting effort for POC. The company was simply outmatched by its competitors because it could not offer the same compensation or benefits. Besides, to implement another plan would be too expensive, and the company currently was suffering from a downturn in its financial results. It was a critical time, and LLC needed to focus on the bottom line.

Alas, LLC was convinced that its managers had given their best efforts to diversify its workforce by hiring POC. The LLC executives were comforted in their disappointment by being in great company. Other large organizations throughout the land of Corporate America were having similar issues in retaining POC.

Several years later, LLC still wondered why so many of its retention strategies had failed. For example, why had POC on the recruiting and retention committee not taken a greater interest? Why had these POC not personally reached out to persuade others to stay? In fact, some POC on the committee had left as well!

Five years after the massive diversity recruiting efforts, the company still had a dismal retention rate for POC, a problem that it had been unable to resolve. After scores of meetings, reports, and presentations, LLC was still wondering, "How could such good intentions go awry?"

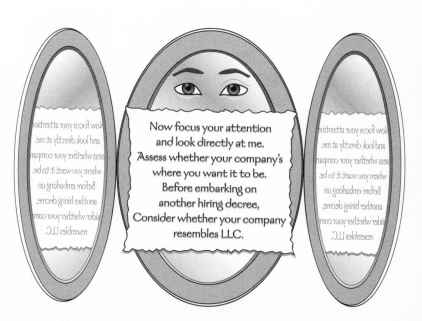

CHAPTER 2

An Inside Look at Lessons Learned Corporation

LESSONS LEARNED CORPORATION, INC. (LLC), orchestrated and implemented a comprehensive and highly effective recruitment strategy, but then something went awry. The fact that LLC was a financially sound company with subsidiaries around the world suggests that the company was accustomed to dealing successfully with organizational challenges, whether financial, operational, or human resources in nature. However, when LLC was faced with challenges around how POC were treated, note how the company responded to the concerns from POC—with disbelief, disclaimers, disappointment, and discouragement—and by shifting focus and responsibility.

While this may not have been the normal way that LLC reacted to organizational challenges, it became the pattern for responding to POC retention issues. This shift from the company's normally astute "problem-solving" approach to one of "wringing hands and gnashing teeth," suggests that leaders may not have been adequately prepared to work with and manage POC. Recognizing the need to have POC on board and pouring money into massive recruitment efforts did not prepare managers to address the complex challenges that many POC encountered at work. Now that managers and leaders were operating in a diverse environment, they may not have been aware of the need to view the workplace from other angles or known that there were other angles to see. In either case, when they did not see what POC saw, it led them to respond inappropriately to the issues impacting POC in their organization.

Table 2.1 highlights scenarios from the story of LLC that demonstrate this point. In many instances, managers and POC viewed the same situation, but came to different conclusions regarding what took place and why. As you read this table, pay close attention to the organizational outcomes, both when the managers and POC were in agreement regarding what occurred and when they were not. These observations will allow you to assess the need for obtaining a complete picture of POCs' experiences in organizations in order to retain them.

The Situation	What POC Saw	What Managers and Leaders Saw	Were the Two Views the Same?	Outcomes
LLC recognized the need to recruit POC and started a recruitment campaign.	POC saw the promise of challenging, high-visibility assignments with great perks.	LLC saw POC who were highly ranked, experienced, and impressively credentialed.	Yes	LLC had an outstanding recruiting year.
POC indicated they were not happy with their experiences at LLC and leaders began to investigate.	POC grew tired of the way they were treated by LLC managers (mediocre assignments, the last to be promoted, and minimal recognition), and viewed it as disparate treatment.	LLC thought their treatment of the POC was equitable.	No	Anger and disbelief erupted on both sides.
POC presented examples to support their claims.	POC viewed their examples as open and honest feedback that would result in positive changes in behavior and improvements in the organization.	LLC viewed their previous decisions as legitimate and saw no reason to change. LLC viewed the POCs' complaints as unmerited. "White males are unhappy, too."	No	Neither group's position was understood or accepted by the other. Distrust and suspicion grew on both sides.
LLC arranged official feedback sessions to resolve the issues.	POC viewed the organization as making sincere attempts to understand their situation.	LLC recognized there were potential problems with how LLC treated POC and agreed to correct and monitor the situation.	Yes	All is well for the time being.

Table 2.1. Did Leaders and Managers See What POC Saw?

The Situation	What POC Saw	What Managers and Leaders Saw	Were the Two Views the Same?	Outcomes
LLC made few significant changes.	POC viewed the conditions at LLC as being the same as they had always been.	LLC viewed everything as fine, since there was no additional feedback.	No	POC started to leave LLC.
Exit interviews were conducted with POC by LLC.	POC did not see that there was any point in giving any further feedback (because nothing would change) and decided to give "politically correct" reasons for their departures.	LLC viewed these "politically correct" responses as meaning that there was nothing that the company could have done to prevent the departure of POC.	No	LLC lost their costly recruitment investments.
LLC's public image was tarnished.	POC viewed this image as justified.	Managers and leaders viewed this image as unfair.	No	LLC was forced to take action.
LLC hired a consulting firm to conduct post-exit interviews with POC.	Since these POC were no longer with LLC, they viewed it as safe to reveal the real reasons why they left LLC. (No, they had not been candid during the exit interviews.)	LLC viewed these POC as hiring "mistakes." They rationalized that the POC were not as sharp as they first believed. They were not meeting performance goals, and they were overly sensitive.	No	There were no changes in the managers' behaviors.

Table 2.1. Did Leaders and Managers See What POC Saw? *continued*

The Situation	What POC Saw	What Managers and Leaders Saw	Were the Two Views the Same?	Outcomes
LLC proceeded with business as usual.	The remaining POC saw that there was no change in LLC's commitment.	LLC concluded that they had ultimately weeded out the hiring mistakes that were normal for any company.	No	The exodus of POC continued until all but a few were gone.
Leaders at LLC wondered, "What happened?"	POC viewed managers and leaders at LLC as being in denial and disingenuous in posing this question.	LLC viewed turnover as a fact of corporate life. There was nothing that they could have done differently.	No	Each group considered the other as being out of touch with reality.
LLC decided to change its strategy and recruit POC from competitor companies instead of from college campuses.	New POC at LLC viewed LLC as a good place to work.	LLC beamed and considered its new recruitment strategy a roaring success.	Yes	All is well for a while.
LLC formed task forces of POC to recruit and retain other POC.	The POC thought that LLC was making a genuine attempt to change its ineffective practices.	The managers thought they had changed, too.	Yes	All is still well.

Table 2.1. Did Leaders and Managers See What POC Saw? *continued*

The Situation	What POC Saw	What Managers and Leaders Saw	Were the Two Views the Same?	Outcomes
Complaints about mediocre assignments and biased treatment resurfaced.	POC felt the situation at LLC was hopeless.	LLC viewed the situation as "the way it was meant to be." LLC needed to turn all its attention to "the bottom line."	No	POC retention at LLC continued to decline.
LLC acknowledged that the environment was not nurturing for POC.	POC viewed this assessment as "old" information.	LLC viewed the situation as discouraging and hopeless.	No	There were no repercussions for the managers involved.
Leaders at LLC focused on the fact that other companies had retention problems too.	POC concluded that the actions of the LLC executives and managers did not demonstrate value for their skills and credentials, their feedback, or their potential.	LLC executives and managers concluded that, even with its retention problems, LLC was still a great company.	No	What do you think?

Table 2.1. Did Leaders and Managers See What POC Saw? *continued*

Questions from the Mirror to the Reader . . .

Consider each situation from Table 2.1 as you respond to the questions that follow.

1. Did LLC executives and managers see what POC saw most often, fairly often, or rarely?

2. When they did not see what POC saw, what were the outcomes? Were they positive or negative?

3. Based on the fact that POC and their managers saw so many things differently, what would you have expected LLC's leadership to do?

4. What do you think were the ultimate consequences of LLC's recruitment effort for POC?

   - Within the organization
   - Outside the organization

5. Whatever your response to the above questions, consider the following. LLC was unable to retain POC because the leadership:

- Didn't understand the discontent on the part of POC, since everything they heard from their managers seemed plausible
- Didn't recognize that they were not viewing the situation in its totality
- Didn't know what to do, since they were used to being successful in dealing with problems in the organization
- Didn't understand that the issues were deep and systemic and that turnover was simply the end result

WHAT WENT WRONG?

In the past, managers at LLC operated in an environment characterized by little or no employee diversity. In this traditional environment, they were evaluated based on their ability to master three competencies: (1) learning the technical applications of the job; (2) contributing to the bottom line (making a profit); and (3) managing business situations in an effective and politically astute manner.

As POC were recruited into the company and the environment became more diverse, managers were not required to update their skills to manage culturally diverse relationships. In fact, neither the company nor the managers recognized that an additional set of management skills was required. The managers were not accustomed to examining their thoughts and feelings about having POC in their organization, their beliefs about what POC were capable of contributing, or the impact that their personal beliefs about POC would have on their ability to evaluate POCs' performance objectively. Additionally, they failed to recognize how their thoughts might impact their ability to establish effective relationships with POC.

Furthermore, managers did not realize that POC might have needs that were different from their own in the workplace. While all employees had a need for mentors and sponsors, information on unwritten rules, avenues for candid feedback, inclusion on key projects, recognition for their accomplishments, and exposure to senior management, people of color were having greater difficulty gaining access to these development channels. Since managers were unaware of this challenge, they never considered providing assistance to people of color in gaining this access. Had they done so, they may have drawn different conclusions about how to manage POC effectively, made different choices, and experienced different outcomes. Instead, their limited insight led them to continue managing POC as they always had—with disastrous results.

CHAPTER 3

Getting an Accurate Reflection

IN ORDER TO MANAGE EFFECTIVELY IN TODAY'S WORKPLACE environment, managers must have the ability to see their employees' real needs, their potential, and their expectations from all angles, unobstructed and unbiased. Yet this same environment, which has become increasingly diverse, also has become increasingly rushed and hurried. As a result, the *first,* the *most accessible,* the *familiar,* or the *stereotypical* view of any employee's situation is what most managers rely on most often.

To use one of these views alone is the same as looking in the mirror head on and seeing only one's face. In this case, you've missed your profile from both sides, and, most importantly, the full view of your body at one time from all the angles. Your face may have looked great, giving you a sense of comfort and confidence. Nonetheless, the rest of you may need significant attention. It is only when you examine your image in its totality that you discover how you really appear to others. Any other data that is collected from the mirror is distorted because it is incomplete.

Incomplete Views That Lead to Accepting "Face" Value	How They Work	Examples
First View	Whoever gets to me first shapes my opinion.	Someone else offers, "Let me tell you what's going on. From what I understand the person overreacted."
Most Accessible View	Quick and easy. May have gathered info as they were passing by.	You stop someone and say, "Hold on. You're in that department aren't you? What's going on?"
Familiar View	It's what your experience has been.	You explain to others, "I experienced the same thing when I came on board, and it wasn't that big of a deal. You have to learn to manage through situations like this."
Stereotypical View	What typically happens in situations like this.	You remind yourself, "Whenever we get a new manager, he or she goes through the same thing. But this employee is taking everything personally and is letting emotions get in the way."

Table 3.1. Incomplete Views and Their Effect

In organizations, a significant amount of data could be gathered if they viewed themselves from all angles. What prevents them from looking at the whole picture is that organizations attempt to use the same approach to issues in the newly diverse environment that they've used in their former non-diverse work environments. The result is that they may not ask the right questions, probe for relevant information, or interpret feedback accurately. Thus, their view is very limited, which leads them to inaccurate conclusions and inappropriate solutions.

WHY PEOPLE OF COLOR LEAVE

Because managers do not have a complete understanding of the issues facing people of color in organizations, the explanations that POC provide regarding why they are leaving the organization often seem plausible and reasonable, for example, "I had a better opportunity" or "This is not a good social climate." But to demonstrate the point that these are often not the real reasons for the departure of POC from organizations, consider the summary of issues and concerns POC shared in candid settings. The list below is compiled from focus group and exit interview data gathered during consulting assignments.

Issues That Prompted People of Color to Leave

- How they were treated personally
- Whether or not they felt valued
- Whether they were guided, coached, or mentored
- Whether their skills were utilized
- Whether they were acknowledged, rewarded, or promoted
- Whether they felt they had support in the organization
- Whether they perceived that there were advancement opportunities for them in the organization
- The opinions of colleagues

A company leader may be quite surprised to hear that "how I was treated by my manager" is the "real" reason that a person of color left the organization, when they had previously been told "I had a job offer that I just couldn't refuse." When one person of color was asked during a third-party exit interview about the discrepancy between his real reason for departure and what he told the company, he explained, "What I said was true. It was an incredible offer. However, I would never have entertained the headhunter's call had I felt good about my chances for success and the relationship with my manager. Still, I didn't want to burn bridges on my way out the door."

This desire not to burn bridges is often the reason that companies do not receive the complete story on why people of color leave. In fact, the explanations people of color provide the company during their exit interviews are often the very same as explanations provided by any other employee. Because the explanations are not unusual, the company does not perceive that there is anything out of the ordinary about the person of color's departure. Yet, since the explanations are incomplete, they are misleading. Without full and accurate information regarding why POC really leave, managers often fail to realize that additional steps are necessary to ensure that POC experience equitable treatment in the workplace.

In fact, when asked about the experiences of POC, many corporate managers respond in a fashion similar to the goldfish in the following anecdote.

Someone once asked a goldfish, "How's the water?" The goldfish replied, "What water?"

Like the goldfish in this anecdote, managers and leaders can become so accustomed to the workplace environment that they assume that everyone shares the same organizational experiences that they are having. Therefore, responses that are similar to those they've heard from employees like themselves (majority employees) seem reasonable. If leaders and managers have benefited from positive experiences, they may respond like the goldfish in the water. They may be so comfortable in the workplace that they don't notice that the POC find it so uncomfortable and unwelcoming that they want to get out. With this great divide between the way that leaders and managers experience the organization and the way that people of color experience the organization, it is difficult for managers to effectively address the issues of people of color.

The next four examples demonstrate how easily managers who are experiencing a comfortable environment may misinterpret feedback from a person of color who is experiencing difficulty in the same work environment.

Example 1

- POC: "I'm leaving the organization to start the family business."

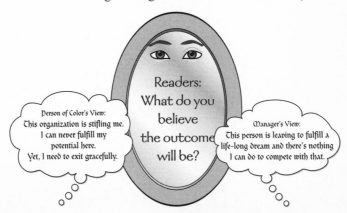

Example 2

- POC: "I'm not being rewarded for my contributions."

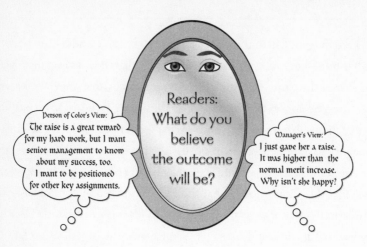

Example 3

- Manager: "In another year you should be ready to move to the next level."

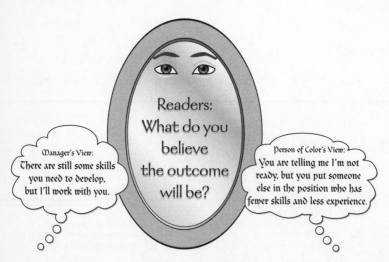

Example 4

- POC: "This environment is not very inclusive."

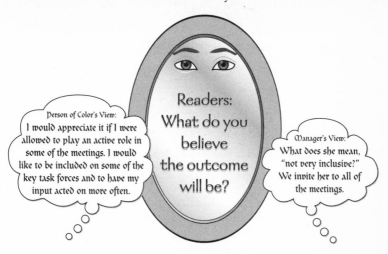

Some managers and leaders may feel that they are relating well to POC and providing appropriate guidance, support, and development. Others may not be comfortable seeking feedback on how well they are managing POC. Since the skill in managing POC varies, it is critical that managers address this important question in each scenario: "What will be the outcome if this person of color doesn't see the situation the same as I do, and if the person of color doesn't view my efforts as being supportive?" As indicated on an earlier chart, what prompts people of color to leave most often is their perception of how they are treated. As you can see from the previous example, managers often have no idea of how their developmental efforts are viewed by the POC they manage. Had the managers been privy to this feedback, they may have adjusted their behavior in order to manage people of color more appropriately. On the other hand, when POC perceive that their managers are not providing them with what they need to succeed, or with what they provide to others in the organization, they often exit the organization in search of a more desirable work environment.

What Happened When One Man Suddenly Saw What Others Saw

One gentleman shared a story of how he meticulously combed his hair forward each day to cover his balding spot. Then one day he saw a video clip from a company sales meeting that showed the back of his head. He concluded, in his own words, that he looked RIDICULOUS! He never combed his hair over again.

As in this example, if managers and leaders take the time to view their decisions, communications, actions, and interactions from this "back of the head" angle, they too may make the decision to never behave in this manner again.

The Steps That Lead to Retention

Many organizations have concluded that recruiting POC is the first and most important step in creating an effective diversity process. However, before recruitment begins, organizations must create a foundation that values people of color, if they want to retain them for the long-term. Only after this foundation is established can organizations effectively implement the steps that lead to the retention of POC:

1. Attracting and hiring POC;

2. Relating to and managing POC;

3. Developing POC; and

4. Rewarding and promoting POC.

If an organization wants to hire and retain POC, it must first create the appropriate culture that "values" people of color before proceeding with any retention initiative. This includes a full assessment of the organization's culture, recruiting, and management practices. Based on their candid assessment of all these factors, managers and leaders must modify their practices to effectively manage all employees, including POC. Only then will they be able to create a company culture where POC can be successful and want to remain. This concept of creating a foundation of "valuing" POC is discussed in detail in the next two chapters.

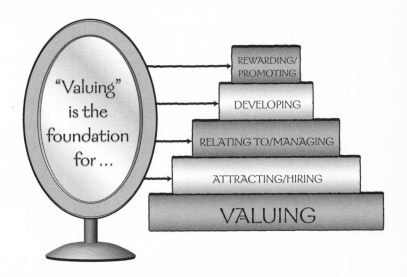

Do You See What I See? Copyright © 2005 by John Wiley & Sons, Inc. Reproduced by permission of Pfeiffer, an imprint of Wiley. www.pfeiffer.com.

CHAPTER 4

Valuing

The Foundation of Retention

"VALUING" IS THE MOST CRITICAL STEP IN
RETAINING PEOPLE of color. It is the
lynchpin or deal breaker in the
entire diversity process. An organization may have diversity strategies and initiatives targeted for
people of color. However, if managers and leaders do not behave
in a manner that respects and
appreciates the very individuals for
whom these initiatives are designed,
the entire process is doomed to fail.

Developing an
elaborate retention
strategy that omits
the "valuing" component
is like designing a
house that has no
foundation.

VALUING: A MEANINGLESS MANTRA?

"Valuing," the foundation of an organization's overall retention process, requires managerial action. It is not enough for a manager to "say" that he or she values people of color. Leaders and managers must behave as if they value people of color. Furthermore, they must be consistent in demonstrating value for these individuals throughout their tenure, not just during the formal recruiting process. Although organizations expend significant time and energy creating and communicating "value" statements, they fail to recognize that individual behavior, not statements, determines the extent to which employees feel valued in the organization.

Nonetheless, demonstrating "value" for diversity is easier said than done. If you are a manager or leader, begin by asking and honestly responding to the following question: "Do I value individuals who are different from myself as much as I do those who are most like me?" Then ask: "Do I value people of color the same as I do other employees in the organization?" Before bristling at the implications of these questions and before hurriedly assuring yourself, "Of course I do," consider that people of color frequently list "not being valued" as the reason that they leave organizations. In fact, the term "value" has been so overused that we say it without considering its meaning and impact. Consider how often you hear the following statements:

- You are a *valued* member of the team;

- Your contributions are *invaluable*;

- We *value* hard work in this organization;

- I think that this product is *value-added*;

- This is a *valuable* tool;

- People are our most *valuable* asset;

- We *value* honesty and integrity; and

- We *value* all our employees.

Leaders and managers use these statements with great frequency, but often that's where they stop. Little consideration is given to whether their daily behaviors are consistent with their "valuing" statements. Even with the overuse of the term, people of color share experiences where value is not evidenced in their daily interactions with management. From their perspective, valuing has become a meaningless mantra. Consider the story of Adil.

Adil was the senior researcher on a product team assigned to update the packaging for one of the company's most popular products. The process had gone extremely well, and Adil was credited with driving the team to explore innovative and creative solutions that exceeded everyone's expectations. The entire team was scheduled to present the new packaging for final approval in seven days. Adil's boss invited him to lunch and opened the conversation with the following: "Adil, I want you to be open-minded about what I'm about to say. Everyone knows that you are the leader of this team and the driving force behind the innovative concepts for this project. It's outstanding work, and I want you to know that we value you and your contributions. However, I'm planning to ask Jason to take the lead in the presentation. I need you to support me in this, and keep in mind that our main objective is to get the new packaging approved. If we do, we all meet our objectives. The reality is that the vice presidents of packing, R&D, and sourcing will be on the panel. Jason has presented to them before and they are very comfortable with him. Sometimes when you become excited about an idea, your accent becomes more detectable. I understand you and don't have a problem with it, but I'm not sure that's the case with these guys. Don't worry, you'll be in the room, and you will get the credit for leading the team."

In Adil's scenario the manager used the term valuing, but the question is whether or not he demonstrated valuing behaviors. What do you believe is Adil's perception of his value at this moment? What message do you believe the manager is sending to Adil's teammates in terms of his value? What message do you think will be communicated to the panel of reviewers?

An organization demonstrates whether or not it values people of color in many ways. The Organizational Reflection Checklist that follows provides some examples. It illustrates at each step of the retention process (from attracting and hiring to rewarding and promoting) what an organizational environment that values people of color reflects and what it reflects when it does not. Additionally, it will help you understand how POC most likely view your organization. We recommend that you take the time to assess the situation at your company by completing the Organizational Reflection Checklist, which begins on the following page.

ORGANIZATIONAL REFLECTION CHECKLIST

Instructions: Read the question in the first column and answer "Yes" or "No" based on the sample descriptions provided in columns 2 and 3. If, in your candid assessment, you have checked "No" for several of the descriptions, ask yourself why these situations exist, what impact they have on your organization, and what should be done to correct the situations.

Question for Reflection	Your Organization May Answer "Yes" If . . .	Your Organization Should Answer "No" If . . .
Are you attracting and hiring POC?	☐ POC are regarded as much of an asset as other employees. ☐ Leaders and managers appreciate the skills, perspectives, and contributions that POC bring to the workplace. ☐ Success factors are realistically and clearly described to POC during the recruitment process. ☐ The organizational environment is one that current POC employees enjoy.	☐ POC must be overqualified to be considered viable candidates for positions. ☐ New POC voice concerns about assignments soon after arrival. ☐ Current POC voice concerns about not being assigned meaningful roles. ☐ There are few or no exciting growth opportunities for POC planned, beyond the initial orientation period. ☐ Former employees are not interested in returning to the organization, even for better positions.

Are you ATTRA HIRI

What are our "success factors" @ BEB Board?

Organizational Reflection Checklist, *continued*

Question for Reflection	Your Organization May Answer "Yes" If...	Your Organization Should Answer "No" If...
Are you relating to POC?	☐ POC say that the organization's programs, policies, and practices designed to encourage cross-cultural relations are effective. ☐ Most people of color testify that the organization's stated commitment to diversity is positively reinforced by the way managers and employees relate to them. ☐ Employees in the organization move beyond being "politically correct" to emulate inclusive behaviors that they see modeled by leaders and managers. ☐ Members of the organization are willing to go beyond racial discomfort, barriers, and affiliations to form relationships that will allow them to get to know POC. For example, diverse groups of people are seen voluntarily interacting with one another in informal settings.	☐ Policies are adhered to more or less strictly when dealing with POC compared with other employees. ☐ Stereotypes are used to predict what POC will like or dislike in both their personal and professional lives. ☐ Leaders have trouble identifying the skills, needs, and interests of POC. ☐ POC are not supported as they seek to observe their cultural traditions. ☐ Members of the organization sidestep conflicts with POC instead of talking and working through them. ☐ Racial dynamics are ignored in conflict situations. ☐ Racial dynamics are exaggerated in conflict situations. ☐ POC are not interested in providing managers and leaders with open feedback.

Are you RELATING to POC?

Organizational Reflection Checklist, *continued*

Question for Reflection	Your Organization May Answer "Yes" If...	Your Organization Should Answer "No" If...
Are you developing POC?	☐ POC receive candid and timely feedback. ☐ POC understand the subtle, unwritten rules of the organization. ☐ POC are pushed to develop new skills, are encouraged to seek new opportunities and experiences, and are satisfied with the level of resources and support that they receive from leaders, managers, and other employees. ☐ POC are afforded the same chance to learn from and move beyond mistakes as their counterparts.	☐ Developmental issues are identified, but not discussed with POC. ☐ When compared with other employees, POC are truly not ready to move into key assignments. ☐ POC are disproportionately underrepresented on succession plans. ☐ Managers hold POC accountable for unwritten rules but never counsel them on the rules. ☐ Few if any POC are in key assignments.

Do You See What I See? Copyright © 2005 by John Wiley & Sons, Inc. Reproduced by permission of Pfeiffer, an imprint of Wiley. www.pfeiffer.com.

Organizational Reflection Checklist, *continued*

Question for Reflection	Your Organization May Answer "Yes" If...	Your Organization Should Answer "No" If...
Are you rewarding and promoting?	☐ POC receive positive feedback on a job well done and are rewarded in a manner that is consistent with how other employees are rewarded and promoted in the organization. ☐ POC are well represented in senior leadership roles in the organization. ☐ Objective measures for rewarding performance are consistently practiced with all employees, including POC. ☐ Compensation packages for POC are comparable to those provided to their counterparts performing at the same level.	☐ POC receive little or no feedback for a job well done, but they receive instant feedback on poor performance. ☐ The work of POC is scrutinized more carefully than that of their counterparts. ☐ POC are in positions that under-utilize their scope and depth of experiences. ☐ When POC are successful, the success is attributed to the group. When their counterparts are successful, the success is attributed to the individual and group. ☐ POC are concentrated in stereotypical staff roles, often including community affairs, recruiting, and diversity. ☐ All or most leaders in the organization share the same cultural profile.

Are you REWARDING AND PROMOTING POC?

So how good do you look? What image is your organization reflecting to others? Is it well on the way to demonstrating value for POC, or is it challenged in critical areas? If you had a number of "no" responses on the Organizational Reflection Checklist, it is time for members of your organization to take a very close look in the mirror and answer the next question honestly: *"Do we value POC enough to identify and address the real issues that impact them in this organization?"*

If the answer is "yes," then the place to start is not with more recruitment plans, organization activities, and public relations strategies. Begin by focusing on individual behaviors. After all, organizations are made up of individuals, and retention cannot be adequately addressed until individuals demonstrate valuing behaviors.

What should managers do to demonstrate that they value people of color? There is no single answer. Appropriate actions will vary based on the circumstances and individuals involved. It is important, therefore, that you understand and appreciate the specific concerns and needs of the person of color with whom you are dealing. At the same time, key behavioral criteria form the foundation of valuing, regardless of the circumstances. They include exhibiting behaviors that demonstrate:

a. Respect, esteem, and consideration for people of color;

b. Appreciation for the talent and skill of people of color;

c. Appreciation for the contributions of people of color;

d. Commitment to the success of people of color; and

e. A sense of realism about people of color.

Of course these criteria should be applied to all applicants and employees, regardless of race, age, gender, or other difference. When these behaviors are genuinely demonstrated with all applicants and employees, "valuing" will be evident, and managers' positive images of the organization will be shared by everyone, including POC. Thus it is important that you question whether you, in your organizational role, are demonstrating valuing behaviors as you pursue the four steps to retention. The valuing behaviors that are described in the remainder of this chapter will help answer that question for you.

INDIVIDUAL VALUING BEHAVIORS

What are the *individual behaviors* that impact retention? An extensive list of the types of individual actions that demonstrate to POC that they are valued follows. As you read through these behaviors, take this opportunity to view yourself. Consider whether you or other leaders or managers are taking these actions and how people of color perceive your

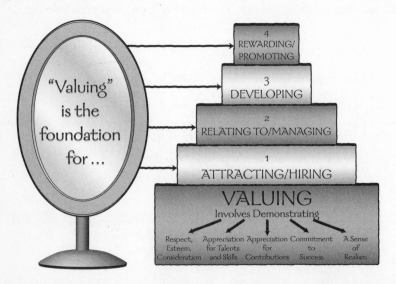

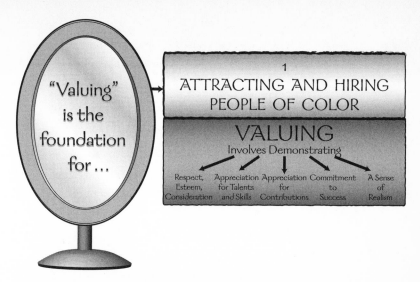

Do You See What I See? Copyright © 2005 by John Wiley & Sons, Inc. Reproduced by permission of Pfeiffer, an imprint of Wiley. www.pfeiffer.com.

behaviors. Remember, you will have the best opportunity to retain POC if you strive to see what POC most likely see.

Retention Step 1: Attracting and Hiring People of Color

If you want to retain the individuals you recruit, valuing must be an integral part of your attracting and hiring process. Consider whether you and others are demonstrating value for people of color during recruitment. As you attempt to attract and hire. . .

**Step 1
to Retention**

> **a. Are You Demonstrating Respect, Esteem, and Consideration for People of Color by**

> ❑ Engaging in a respectful manner with people of color throughout the hiring process? (For example: Exploring with these candidates how they will

"complement" the organization, rather than focusing only on how they will "fit in"? Respecting their cultural protocol by not scheduling interviews on days that might conflict with their cultural observances?)

❏ Utilizing the same hiring processes for people of color as for other prospective employees? and

❏ Asking questions that are appropriate, not intrusive personal questions? (Intrusive questions include inquiries unrelated to their ability to perform in the position.)

b. Are You Demonstrating Appreciation for the Talent and Skill of People of Color by

❏ Offering assignments commensurate with their experience, talent, and skills?

❏ Offering compensation packages that are in line with other employees with similar histories? and

❏ Describing to them what they can realistically expect once they are on board in terms of assignments, upward mobility, support, opportunities, and work environment?

Deliberately creating the wrong impression by sharing information that is unrealistic or by omitting critical details in order to meet recruiting goals can have a negative effect. People of color will soon discover the organizational reality, and the inaccurate representations will lead to disillusionment and distrust, impacting retention and the organization's reputation. Consider the following story.

All That Glitters...

A gentleman who had lived a long and productive life became ill suddenly and passed away. At the end of his passage he was greeted by Saint Peter, who said, "Welcome to our holding station." "Holding station?" the gentleman asked. "Yes," the Archangel said. "This is where you get to choose." "Choose between what?" the man asked, perplexed. "Well, this is where you choose between Heaven and Hell." The gentleman was startled. He assumed that he was bound for Heaven because he had lived such a good life. Besides, why would anyone choose to go to Hell?

He asked the Archangel, "Do many people select Hell over Heaven?" The Archangel replied, "Yes, a good number make this choice." Surprised, the gentleman asked, "Why?" The Archangel responded, "I can't tell you why, but I'll give you the same option that I give to everyone else. You can visit each for a day, then select your final destination." This seemed reasonable to the gentleman, and he agreed to take the Archangel up on the offer.

His first preview was of Heaven. When he arrived, he was astounded and overwhelmed. Heaven was beautiful beyond anything he could describe. He could think of no words that would do justice to the beauty and tranquility of Heaven. He was sure that this would be his choice. Nonetheless, it would not hurt to take a look at Hell, particularly since the visit was scheduled already. Besides, he was curious as to why others had selected Hell. As he was leaving Heaven on his way to Hell, he saw the Archangel and gave him a thumbs-up sign. "I'll be back soon to give you my decision, the gentleman said." "Very well," said the Archangel.

When he reached Hell, he was astounded again. It too was beautiful. It was different from Heaven in that the atmosphere was much more dynamic. There were parties, banquets, sports events—any type of activity that you could imagine. Additionally, a group had been assigned to meet him as he walked through the door and serve as his hosts for the visit. The group was warm and friendly and welcomed him with open arms. They spent the day describing what life would be like here, as opposed to the more serene environment of Heaven. When they discovered that he was a sports enthusiast, they told him about opportunities to become head of one of Hell's sports teams. The day had been so enjoyable that he was sad when it was over.

On his way back up to meet the Archangel, the gentleman was in a quandary. Throughout his life he had aspired to go to Heaven, but Hell was not at all as he had been led to believe. The residents of Hell had impressed him with their warm reception and with the interest they had shown in his joining them. Additionally, the activities that they described, especially the sports activities, were more to his liking. He had always enjoyed an active life, and he wasn't sure how well he would deal with the peace and tranquility that Heaven offered.

By the time he reached the Archangel, the gentleman had made up his mind. He, like many others, would choose Hell over Heaven. When he shared his decision, the Archangel asked, "Are you sure? You realize that, once you make this choice, you cannot change your mind and come back to Heaven?" "Yes, I'm sure. Heaven is wonderful beyond words. But Hell seems to be more suited to my aspirations. They have promised me opportunities to grow. I want to thank you for this wonderful opportunity to preview Heaven, however. The Archangel offered him a resigned smile and wished him well. Then he walked the gentleman over to the road leading to the gates of Hell and said, "Farewell, my friend."

On his way to Hell, he was thrilled to begin his after-life in such an exciting place. Upon arrival at the doors of Hell, he paused for a few seconds thinking about how wonderfully things had turned out. With delightful anticipation he knocked on the door and prepared to enter. After a brief pause the door slid open. Rushing through the gates, he came to an abrupt halt. This did not remotely resemble the place he had visited the day before.

There was smog and smoke everywhere. The residents were barely visible, but he knew they were there because of the loud cries, moans, and wails. There were fights, disagreements, and chaos. There were no parties, nor any sporting events. There was no beauty. He could not find anyone he recognized. Individuals he asked about the activities he had previewed the day before knew nothing of them. Finally, he ran into one person who had been part of his welcoming committee on the day before. He ran over to the person and asked frantically, "What happened? Where is the place that I saw yesterday? Where are the food, the sports events, and the laughter? Where am I?" The person looked at him with an astonished expression and replied, "Oh, you didn't know? Yesterday was different. We were recruiting. Today is business as usual."

—Adaptation of Internet Humor (original author unknown)

Although versions of this story have been told many times across Corporate America as an amusing anecdote, it reflects an unfortunate reality described by many people of color recruited into organizations. Once they commit to the organization, the reality of their experience is so different from what was described that it creates a sustained sense of distrust.

There is, however, one major factor in their experience that differs from the anecdote. They are not eternally committed to "Hell," as was this gentleman. They can and do leave these organizations through the "revolving door," which adversely impacts the company's financial results, reputation, and retention outcomes. Now let's return to your assessment of your organization.

c. Are You Demonstrating Appreciation for the Contributions of People of Color by

❑ Taking into consideration their previous experience and accomplishments?

❑ Not requiring people of color to repeatedly prove themselves at lower levels when they have already proven their skills and when they are capable of contributing at more significant levels? and

❑ Being receptive to the idea, as well as optimistic, that these individuals will contribute in a meaningful way to the organization? (This involves having an attitude of expectation rather than an attitude of skepticism and doubt.)

d. Are You Demonstrating Commitment to the Success of People of Color by

❑ Taking their goals and aspirations into consideration and collaborating with them to ensure that their placement is in line with what they would like to achieve in their careers?

❑ Staying involved after the formal recruiting process is over and they are on board—not simply disappearing, never to be heard from again (for example, touching base periodically over lunch, a cup of coffee, or by phone)?

❑ Displaying the same level of friendliness and sense of concern as you demonstrated during the recruiting process (please do not change from the Mr. or Ms. "Wonderful Engaging Personality" to "I Don't Quite Remember You" when you see the person of color later in the corridor.)? and

❑ Taking the time to offer assistance in the person's orientation and transition and to provide basics on survival skills and unwritten rules peculiar to your organizational culture? (Insights about organizational nuances, such as how reports should be presented; people to consult before making presentations; and so on are important in the orientation process. A client once mentioned how a new hire got off on the wrong foot when he made his presentation in a portrait format rather than a landscape format, as was the custom in their organization. This might have been avoided if he had received an orientation on unwritten rules of the organization.)

e. Are You Demonstrating a Sense of Realism About People of Color by

❑ Examining your beliefs about people of color who are currently in the organization, addressing their developmental needs, and fully utilizing their skills? (Keep in mind that the people of color you are attempting to attract will seek information about the success of people of color who are currently in the organization. Through their own networks they will gather facts about achievements, placement, and status of other people of color in the organization. Their assessment of *what has happened* has a greater impact on their decision to join the organization than promises from leaders and managers regarding *what will happen* for them personally.)

❑ Requiring the same or similar credentials from POC as you do from other candidates being considered for the position; not seeking "super minorities," those with credentials, experience, and skills far beyond what is needed for the role—and far beyond what other non-minority candidates would be required to demonstrate? and

❑ Offering compensation packages to people of color that are the same as or commensurate with packages offered to their non-minority counterparts?

As you seek to attract and hire people of color, are you demonstrating that you value them? Are other leaders and managers of your organization doing so? How do you think people of color would respond to the questions above?

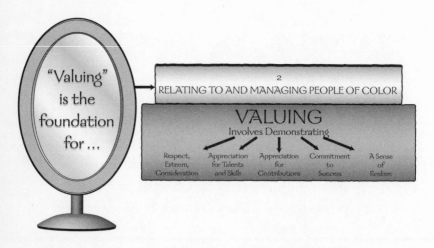

Retention Step 2: Relating to and Managing People of Color

In order to effectively manage anyone, including people of color, you must first be able to relate to them. This involves connecting and sharing on a one-on-one level and understanding and caring about the issues that matter to them. The question is whether you are developing and cultivating relationships that allow you to effectively connect with the people of color you manage. As you attempt to relate to and manage people of color. . .

**Step 2
to Retention**

a. Are You Demonstrating Respect, Esteem, and Consideration for the People of Color by

❑ Getting to know their personal values and concerns, comforts, and discomforts, what energizes and inspires them, and staying on top of how these factors change for them over time (the things someone found inspiring two years ago may seem insignificant today)?

❑ Offering support (even if it is just listening) when there is discord in your organization? (If you have done a good job of understanding people's comforts and discomforts, you will be more sensitive to when they need support.)

❑ Honoring their need for "belonging" to the organization as well as their need to be recognized as individuals with "individual" needs and interests? and

❑ Engaging in discussions and activities that both of you enjoy or find meaningful?

b. Are You Demonstrating Appreciation for the Talent and Skills of People of Color by

- ❑ Interacting with them on a one-to-one basis in order to become familiar with their skills, rather than relying on hearsay, opinions, or written reports?
- ❑ Becoming familiar with the variety of leadership positions that they hold outside of work and utilizing those leadership abilities in the workplace?
- ❑ Allowing them freedom to do their work without looking over their shoulders?
- ❑ Avoiding any tendency to second-guess and undermine the decisions they have made with their subordinates or colleagues? and
- ❑ Encouraging them to use their talents and skills in creative ways (even if it is not your usual way of doing things)?

c. Are You Demonstrating Appreciation for the Contributions of People of Color by

- ❑ Asking for and taking into consideration their perceptions and opinions and taking time to try to understand differences in perceptions that you may have?
- ❑ Avoiding any tendency to discount differences in perception and assuming that the differences will not matter to the person of color or that your way is best?
- ❑ Offering sincere thanks for contributions by pointing to specific things that you appreciate?
- ❑ Showing appreciation in ways that are meaningful to that particular person of color and remembering that not all people of a certain group (Asian, Latino, or others) value the same things? and

❑ Not allowing others to marginalize or minimize their perspectives? (One CEO demonstrated this level of valuing when he publicly supported a creative cost-cutting idea presented by a person of color even after a senior executive had openly discounted the idea.)

d. Are You Demonstrating Commitment to the Success of People of Color by

❑ Knowing specifically how each person of color defines his or her personal success?

❑ Helping all POC understand what it will take to achieve their goals? (This may include such things as understanding the organizational culture, as well as critical skills and networks that need to be developed.)

❑ Talking about ways they wish to contribute to the organization and doing what you can to provide those opportunities? and

❑ Arranging meetings periodically to discuss how they are progressing toward their goals?

e. Are You Demonstrating a Sense of Realism About People of Color by

❑ Appreciating that it is not a threatening situation for people of color to convene in formal or informal settings?

❑ Understanding that people of color are not all alike; they have different values, preferences, ways of communicating, working styles, learning styles, expectations about how things should be done, and methods of managing resources? and

❑ Understanding that discrimination based on race is a reality for many people of color; recognizing that this

reality often creates challenges in the work environment; and accepting that different people of color
handle this challenge in different ways?

As you manage and relate to people of color, are you demonstrating
that you value them? Are other leaders and managers of your organization doing this? How do you think people of color would respond to
these questions?

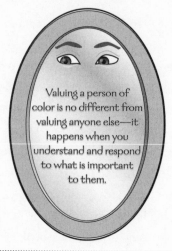

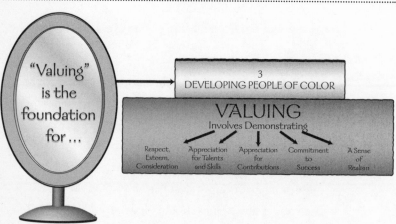

Retention Step 3: Developing People of Color

Managers who perform this step well respect and appreciate talents that people of color offer and help them grow to their full capacity. They are candid and offer timely feedback about performance. They push the individual to develop new skills, provide encouragement in seeking new opportunities and experiences, provide resources and support, and share unwritten rules of the organization. Additionally, such managers recognize the importance of allowing for mistakes and provide the opportunity and support to overcome them. It is important to remember that if you help people of color develop their full potential, the entire organization will benefit. As you are attempting to develop people of color, remember to ask yourself. . .

Step 3 to Retention

a. Are You Demonstrating Respect, Esteem, and Consideration for People of Color by

- ❏ Assuming they are capable of being developed for multiple roles in the organization, including leadership? and
- ❏ Finding out what roles they would like to fill and how they would like to be supported in their development?

b. Are You Demonstrating Appreciation for the Talent and Skills of People of Color by

- ❏ Helping them to further develop the talents and skills that they already have?
- ❏ Encouraging them to train, develop, and mentor others in the organization (and not just other people of color)?

c. Are You Demonstrating Appreciation for the Contributions of People of Color by

❑ Providing entrées so they may showcase their contributions in a broad range of public forums (conferences and keynotes), not just those forums specific to people of color? and

❑ Providing training opportunities such as certifications and degree programs to further enhance and validate their current contributions?

d. Are You Demonstrating Commitment to the Success of People of Color by

❑ Putting them in key assignments?

❑ Providing resources and growth opportunities for them at the same level that you are providing for others?

❑ Providing "stretch" opportunities for them at the same rate that they are provided for others instead of deciding they need "just a little more development" in a lateral position while their colleagues move to higher levels?

❑ Providing support and guidance by sharing candid feedback and information?

❑ Coaching them to address issues that impact their careers?

❑ Treating what the organization may regard as a failed project as a learning experience for the person of color. This includes helping the person analyze the project and what needs to be done differently? and

❑ Exposing them to key people in the organization at the same rate that you do for others?

e. Are You Demonstrating a Sense of Realism About People of Color by

❏ Not assuming that they do not want to be in leadership positions or that they cannot handle them?

❏ Not asking them to teach others to do the jobs that they were denied?

❏ Coaching them to develop their unique abilities while at the same time helping them to understand and thrive in the organizational culture? and

❏ Recognizing that the best people of color will not tarry long in one organization waiting to be recognized and developed? (They will develop themselves; then most will move on to other organizations that will cultivate their growth.)

Are you demonstrating that you value people of color as you seek to develop them? Are other leaders and managers of your organization doing so too? How do you think people of color would respond to these questions?

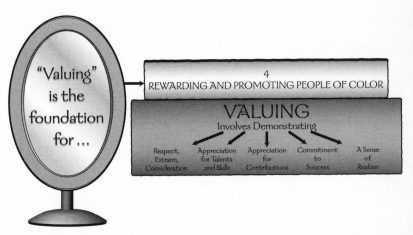

Retention Step 4: Rewarding and Promoting People of Color

Rewards are powerful motivators. Although individuals may experience a personal sense of satisfaction from a job well done, this does not replace the satisfaction gained from positive feedback, recognition, praise, and rewards from other individuals in the organization, particularly organizational leaders. In order for these positive reinforcements to have the appropriate meaning for people of color, they must be *equitable* and *consistent* with the experiences of others within the organization. They cannot be provided haphazardly, sparingly, or belatedly (as was the case at Lessons Learned Corporation). When it comes to rewarding and promoting are you. . .

Step 4 to Retention

a. Demonstrating Respect, Esteem, and Consideration for People of Color by

❏ Taking the time to express appreciation for a job well done?

❏ Asking people of color for their input on matters that are important to the business, even if they do not volunteer?

❏ Looking for short-term projects or assignments that can be used to bolster morale if you sense that a person of color on your team has a momentary lapse in confidence?

❏ Inviting POC to high-level meetings they would not normally attend? and

❏ Exploring ways to engage POC in high-profile tasks?

b. Are You Demonstrating Appreciation for the Talent and Skill of People of Color by

❑ Being consistent in acknowledging the successes of all employees, including people of color (giving credit when and where due)?

❑ Ensuring that employees are rewarded equitably for their outstanding achievements?

❑ Challenging leaders and managers to explain and legitimately justify their decisions if the skills of people of color are overlooked? and

❑ Searching for the hidden and underutilized talents of people of color? (In some cases people of color have been recruited with impressive credentials. Yet they have been placed in roles that are beneath their qualifications. Identify these people of color and seek opportunities to move them into more responsible assignments.)

c. Are You Demonstrating Appreciation for the Contributions of People of Color by

❑ Not allowing others to take credit inappropriately? (A common complaint by people of color is that their ideas are overlooked, then repeated and credited to someone else. Make note of which contributions are made by whom and be sure to publicly acknowledge the individual who initiated the idea. If the person of color has indicated a preference for private recognition, honor that preference. However, never give credit that belongs to one person to someone else.)

❑ Developing informal methods to highlight the accomplishments of your team on a periodic basis (so that all

team members can appreciate one another's contributions)? and

❑ Communicating these contributions to key individuals
outside your area?

d. Are You Demonstrating Commitment to the Success of People of Color by

❑ Highlighting their skills (along with other employees')
to ensure that they are not being overlooked when you
are in meetings to discuss career opportunities, new
assignments, developmental roles, and succession planning? and

❑ Talking with people of color in the company outside
your immediate area who are successful currently and
congratulating them on their success?

e. Are You Demonstrating a Sense of Realism About People of Color by

❑ Reminding leaders and managers that other individuals,
including some current leaders, have had unsuccessful
experiences as part of their career development? (One
of the concerns that we often hear from people of color
in organizations is that unsuccessful experiences are
used to derail their careers. On the other hand, their
colleagues' unsuccessful experiences are considered as
"developmental learning experiences." If their potential
is discounted or minimized because of unsuccessful
experiences, the level of trust between the manager
and the person of color is threatened.)

Are you valuing people of color as you make your reward and promotion decisions? Are other leaders and managers in your organization doing so? How do you think people of color would respond to these questions?

By now you have probably realized at least two important points:
1. "Valuing" is not as simple as the frequent use of the term would suggest.
2. "Valuing" is nevertheless critical, and managers and leaders must assume this ongoing responsibility in order to avoid turnover.

MORE THAN GOOD INTENTIONS

Demonstrating the valuing behaviors described above may present a challenge, even when you have good intentions. The difficulty may not be with your desire to do so, but with making and *keeping* commitments that result in changed behaviors. Changing behaviors is a significant challenge for most of us; and under pressure, change can be especially hard. When tough decisions with no clear-cut solutions demand your attention, the commitment to demonstrate valuing behaviors may be lost. The tendency is to fall back on familiar practices that exclude or marginalize certain groups. Short on time and answers, it may be tempting to do as leaders at Lessons Learned Corporation (LLC) did—repeat the same old practices and hope in vain for different results. Later you may genuinely wonder, "What went wrong? My intentions were good!"

Are you a leader or manager whose good intentions sometimes go awry when dealing with people of color? Or are you familiar enough with valuing behaviors to make decisions that promote retention rather than turnover? The questionnaire in the next chapter is designed to help you make that assessment.

CHAPTER 5

Little Things That Make Us Look . . . Good . . . Bad

A Look at Subtle Behaviors

SOME MANAGEMENT BEHAVIORS ARE OBVIOUSLY INAPPROPRIATE.

Miriam, a college graduate and leader in her community, decided to take an administrative position in a leading hospitality organization in order to get grounded in all aspects of the business. She was enjoying the work and getting a good grasp of things. But Miriam was very concerned with management's practices. Paul, one of the departmental managers, had been particularly patronizing and rude. Among other things, he had demeaned her as he gave her some materials to review by asking, "You can read, can't you?" When Miriam shared the incident with the departmental director, he excused Paul's behavior by saying to Miriam, "Oh, Paul's just being Paul. He makes these types of comments to everyone. Ignore him."

This example sounds "over the top," but it actually happened. Fortunately, people like Paul are a minority. Most individuals are concerned about how their behaviors impact others and will say and do the appropriate thing when the options are clear and easy. But the options are not always clear when managing people and differences. Moreover, the subtle missteps, just like the obvious blunders in Miriam's experience, can raise questions about how much one values people of color. Hence, understanding the subtle differences in perspective is an important element of retaining people of color. The questionnaire that follows will help you determine how well you understand some of these subtleties.

UPON REFLECTION QUESTIONNAIRE

The questionnaire that follows includes ten scenarios based on real diversity situations that have often occurred in corporate environments. It is designed to help you see how different reactions to each scenario can encourage or discourage the retention of POC.

We encourage managers, leaders, diversity practitioners, and others to respond to the questionnaire. Those who have little background in diversity as well as those who are seasoned in it will find the questionnaire useful. If you have a *great deal of experience* in diversity, the answers to the questionnaire may seem obvious. However, you may be able to support others in learning more about the subtleties of managing people from different backgrounds by using the rationales provided.

If you have had *little or moderate experience* with diversity, the choice of responses will provide insight for you (especially since the responses are things that people actually do). However, your greatest learning may come from reading the rationale that accompanies each response.

UPON REFLECTION QUESTIONNAIRE

Instructions: Read through each of the scenarios that follow. Four options are presented for each. Select the option that seems best to you for the long-term interest of employees, your department, and your organization. Record your selections in Column 1 of the Upon Reflection Scoring Sheet, which is on a separate page after the questionnaire.

1. If a person of color complains about unfair treatment in the workplace, you should:

   A. Tell that person you appreciate that he or she shared this perception with you.

   B. Tell that person you will not tolerate discrimination, then attack/confront the person's supervisor.

   C. Tell that person you will not tolerate discrimination. Ask for more information, and then investigate to find out what happens.

   D. Move that person's desk closer to your office so you can watch out for him or her.

2. Your organization has had several EEO charges filed recently. Now you have a person of color who is not performing at the expected level. You should:

   A. Give him or her a "meets expectation" on the performance appraisal anyway to avoid conflict.

   B. Talk to the person of color directly and specifically about the performance issue.

   C. Talk to another person of color to get advice about what you should do.

   D. Share with a colleague how frustrating it is to have a person of color put you in this predicament.

3. One of the managers who reports to you is an excellent performer, but the turnover rates for female POC in her department are very high. You should:

  A. Promote her because her performance warrants it. Put retention in its proper perspective.

  B. Point out to her that her positive results may be offset by the financial losses resulting from turnover.

  C. Move her to another position where she has no supervisory responsibilities.

  D. Tell her that her performance on diversity is not acceptable because her retention numbers have made you look bad.

4. Your company is having problems recruiting and retaining POC. You should:

  A. Hire a recruitment firm that specializes in finding POC.

  B. Tell your managers that you expect each of them to establish a mentoring relationship with at least one person of color within the next quarter.

  C. Conclude there are not enough talented POC available and praise any of your managers who say they have tried unsuccessfully to find and hire POC.

  D. Conduct focus groups to find out why POC are not attracted to your company or why they leave once they have joined the company. Then develop and implement a plan based on what you learn.

5. You read about the whopping settlements from discrimination charges. Your company may be at risk too! You should:

  A. Decide to hire fewer POC to lessen the chances you will be sued too.

B. Talk to companies that have been sued to learn from their mistakes.

C. Call a staff meeting to discuss areas where your company needs to improve. Then develop and implement a plan to reach improvement goals.

D. Communicate to the employees how these settlements hurt the company's bottom line.

6. One of the people who reports to you tells you that she does not think all the company's focus on retaining POC is necessary. She says, "Anyone who has ambition can pull himself up by his bootstraps like I did."
You should:

A. Tell her to go to a cultural event with POC to gain insights into other cultures.

B. Send her a memo indicating that she is being required to attend the next diversity training session.

C. Challenge her to consider the possibility that "ambition" might not be the only factor that impacts POCs' job satisfaction and retention.

D. Accept that you cannot control the way she feels. As long as she treats everyone the same, her actions are okay.

7. A POC who reports to you tells you he gives 120 percent and that he is not interested in learning to play golf or tennis in order to get ahead. You should:

A. Tell him you can appreciate his feeling this way, but explain how and why he may be limiting his opportunities by not participating in these particular sports.

B. Ask him if it would be helpful to invite some other POC to come along.

C. Tell him to get over it because it's not about fun. It's about succeeding. Then tell him that you pretend to enjoy many things that aren't fun for you.

D. Acknowledge that he does give 120 percent, impress on him the need to develop a broader network, and help him brainstorm other ways to expand his network.

8. In a training program, a person of color openly confronts you about your poor record of developing POC. You should:

A. Defend yourself by naming all the POC you know with whom you are friendly.

B. Admit that you need to improve your record. Tell the person you plan to learn as much as possible from the training session and invite him or her to continue giving you feedback.

C. Share an article that spells out why POC leave organizations, which, by the way, are reasons you cannot control.

D. Remind the person that this training program is not supposed to be confrontational. Additionally, let him or her know that he or she has made you uncomfortable. Invite the person to discuss this matter with you privately after the class.

9. One of your best-performing POC tells you she is thinking of leaving. You should:

A. Beg her to stay and offer her a raise.

B. Confide in her that she is on the "high potential" list and that her opportunities will be many if she'll just be patient.

C. Ask her about her experiences at the company and why she is thinking of leaving.

D. Offer to pay for her tuition to attend an MBA school or executive program that requires her to stay with the company for three years after graduation.

10. POC have called the diversity initiative a joke. You should:

A. Develop a diversity checklist to track how much progress you are making.

B. Ask for specific examples that led them to believe that diversity is a "joke." Address the most critical issues immediately.

C. Host a cultural festival and encourage employees to bring ethnic foods and wear ethnic clothing to demonstrate that diversity is important. This will promote goodwill.

D. Send a memo to everyone in the company. The memo should highlight the progress the company has made in its diversity efforts, including positive comments from two or three POC.

UPON REFLECTION SCORING SHEET

Question #	Column 1: Your Response	Column 2: Your Points
	In this column, record the option (A, B, C, or D) that you believe represents the most appropriate course of action for each question.	After recording all ten of your responses, read the answers and rationales provided. Find the number of points corresponding to the options you selected, and record those points in this column.
1		
2		
3		
4		
5		
6		
7		
8		
9		
10		
TOTAL POINTS		

Do You See What I See? Copyright © 2005 by John Wiley & Sons, Inc. Reproduced by permission of Pfeiffer, an imprint of Wiley. www.pfeiffer.com.

SCORING THE UPON REFLECTION QUESTIONNAIRE

The four responses for each scenario have been assigned values from 0 (worst response) to 3 (best response). The Ratings Chart which follows shows how points have been assigned.

1. Read the chart and become familiar with the ratings.

2. Next, review our ratings for each of the scenarios and the explanation for each of the options. Be sure to read the rationales that are provided for all of the options, not just the options you selected.

3. Record the points assigned to your selection (0, 1, 2, or 3) in Column 2 of the scoring sheet.

4. Repeat Steps 2 and 4 until you have scored all ten scenarios.

5. Add your scores and record your total score on the last line of the scoring sheet.

From Our View...

Ratings Chart for
Upon Reflection Questionnaire

Points	Rating Descriptions	Explanation
3	The best of the four responses because you looked in a clear mirror from all angles.	The most appropriate choice of the responses we provided. This is not to suggest that there are not other responses that may be equally appropriate for your situation.
2	The second-best response because the mirror had a little smudge that blocked a key detail.	This response recognizes that some action was taken. It may not be the best action, and there may be pitfalls in this solution. However, the final outcome is more likely to be positive than negative.
1	The third-best response because you glanced at a mirror from only one angle, and the mirror had a glare.	The impact that this action would have on POC was not carefully considered. The final outcome of this action is more likely to be negative than positive.
0	The worst response because you passed by a mirror, but you did not look.	Although some readers may find some of the solutions humorous, some well-meaning leaders, managers, and supervisors have actually taken these actions. These are not effective solutions to the problem, and such actions are very likely to result in negative outcomes.

PREFERRED ANSWERS AND RATIONALE

1. If a person of color complains about unfair treatment in the workplace you should:

  1   A. Tell the individual you appreciate that he or she shared this perception.

  2   B. Tell the POC you will not tolerate discrimination, then confront/attack the person's supervisor.

  3   C. Tell the POC you will not tolerate discrimination, ask for more information, and then investigate to find out what happened.

  0   D. Move that person's desk closer to your office so you can watch out for him or her.

    C. (3 pts.) Our best choice is "C." By telling the person you will not tolerate discrimination, you state your commitment to fair treatment. Asking for more information demonstrates interest in his or her concern; and investigating the claim is the first step to finding a solution to the conflict.

    B. (2 pts.) As mentioned above, telling the person you will not tolerate discrimination sends a clear message, but the attack on the supervisor is almost sure to result in defensiveness or retaliation.

    A. (1 pt.) Telling the person that you appreciate that he or she shared this perception may sound like an encouraging response, but the person hearing it is likely to feel put off. After all, you have not said or done anything to show that you really see his or her point of view or understand what he or she is experiencing. Furthermore, you have not done anything to address the situation.

D. (0 pts.) If your goal is to create an environment in which the person of color feels included and appreciated, moving his or her desk closer to your office is not likely to yield the results that you want. The person of color has not asked you for *protection* from the problem but *correction* of the problem. However, you can't correct the problem without first establishing the "root cause" of the unfair treatment. Your overprotective response is likely to make the problem worse. . . . The person of color is likely to feel uncomfortable under your spotlight of security. . . . Other staff members will wonder what all the fuss is about. . . . The perpetrator(s), who have no idea there is an issue, won't change. . . . Besides, the person of color may feel that you are the source of the problem.

2. Your organization has had several EEO charges filed recently. Now you have a POC who is not performing at the expected level. You should:

0   A.   Give him or her a "meets expectation" on the performance appraisal anyway to avoid conflict.

3   B.   Talk to the person of color directly and specifically about the performance issue.

1   C.   Talk to another person of color to get advice about what you should do.

2   D.   Share with a colleague how frustrating it is to have a person of color put you in this predicament.

B. (3 pts.) The best choice is "B." Talking to the person directly and specifically about his or her performance will help you send a clear message about your expectations. The person of color may not like your view, but it is likely that she or he will appreciate your honesty. Additionally, by being clear and direct, you will have given that person the guidance and feedback that will support his or her professional development.

D. (2 pts.) "D" is our second-best choice since the underperforming person of color has not "put you in this predicament." That person's performance has nothing to do with the EEO charges. On the other hand, there can be an element of value in this choice. Sharing your frustrations with a colleague may not be a bad idea. You will need to understand and sort out your own feelings before you can truly recognize the person of color's needs and give him or her objective developmental feedback and guidance. However, be selective. Limit your sharing to those who are likely to expand your thinking (not someone who thinks just like you) and be open to receiving feedback.

C. (1 pt.) While going to another person of color may provide insight into why this person of color is not performing, disclosing confidential information about an employee's performance is an inappropriate management practice. If discovered, it will likely prevent you from forming a trustful relationship or destroy existing trust. Furthermore, it may raise suspicion and be regarded as a political tactic. If you choose to talk to another manager about the situation, select someone (a person of color or otherwise) with whom you have an established, "trusting" relationship. If the group of people with whom you interact is already diverse, it will be easy for you to identify the right person.

A (0 pts.) "A" serves no one's best interest. Giving the person a "meets expectation" on the performance appraisal to avoid conflict does not encourage a standard of excellence. Furthermore, it shows you are uncomfortable handling this situation directly and candidly. Most importantly, by withholding your candid feedback, you have missed the opportunity to help the person of color improve his or her performance.

3. One of the managers who reports to you is an excellent performer, but the turnover rates for female POC in her department are very high. You should:

   0   A. Promote her because her performance warrants it, and put retention in its proper perspective.

   3   B. Point out to her that her positive results may be offset by the financial losses resulting from turnover.

   2   C. Move her to another position where she has no supervisory responsibilities.

   1   D. Tell her that her performance on diversity is not acceptable because her retention numbers have made you look bad.

   B. (3 pts.) Pointing out how her positive numbers are reduced when the cost of turnover is subtracted will help her understand how managing a diverse workforce can impact financial results. Since your employee is results-oriented, she will have a strong motive for managing her diverse workforce more effectively.

   D. (2 pts.) It is commendable that you have stated clearly that her retention numbers are not acceptable. Yet, by telling her that she made you "look bad," you may discourage rather than motivate an otherwise excellent performer. The first step will be to understand how your personal feelings (being embarrassed about "looking bad") might impact your ability to have a constructive discussion with this employee. In this situation, it is particularly important to keep your emotions under control and to focus on providing helpful feedback.

C. (1 pt.) By moving her to another position where she does not have supervisory responsibilities you will have failed to address two critical questions: (1) Does she have the skill to manage differently when placed in a future supervisory assignment? and (2) Have you managed your responsibility to provide clear and constructive feedback without adversely impacting her performance?

A. (0 pts.) Promoting this performer will send a message throughout the organization that "retaining POC is not a priority." If the organization is having a problem with retention, it is important that the entire organization, including this manager, appreciate the importance of hiring and retaining a diverse workforce. In this case, financial success includes the ability to effectively manage a diverse work group.

4. Your company is having problems recruiting and retaining POC. You should:

   1 A. Hire a recruitment firm that specializes in finding POC.

   2 B. Tell your managers that you expect each of them to establish a mentoring relationship with at least one person of color within the next quarter.

   0 C. Conclude there are not enough talented POC available and praise any of your managers who say they have tried unsuccessfully to find and hire POC.

   3 D. Conduct focus groups to find out why POC are not attracted to your company or why they leave once

they have joined the company. Then develop and implement a plan based on what you learn.

D. (3 pts.) Understanding the organization's climate, strengths, and weaknesses is a management responsibility. Information from the focus groups will help you understand why POC are not attracted to your organization or why employees often leave. By conducting an assessment you will demonstrate your interest in these individuals' concerns and a willingness to listen. The most important element of "D," however, is implementation. Gathering information for the sake of gathering it (and doing nothing with it) promotes cynicism and distrust within the organization. Addressing the employees' concerns will show your commitment to overcoming issues that stand in the way of diversity retention.

B. (2 pts.) Mentoring programs can be valuable for all employees, including POC. However, simply telling managers to "establish mentoring relationships within the next quarter" may not address the problem. Before developing a mentoring program or any other type of program, you will need to find out what the real issues are. Talk to several POC and ask them to give you their views about why you are having trouble recruiting and retaining POC.

A. (1 pt.) Effective recruitment and retention strategies include a wide range of tactics that may mean hiring a recruitment firm that specializes in identifying candidates who are POC. Utilizing outside firms for targeted recruitment is a popular and helpful practice that is used by many organizations. However, it cannot substitute for good internal management practices. Even if the recruitment firm presents an excellent list of diverse candidates, the environment often influences an individual's decision to join the organization. Moreover, it is the organizational environment that will keep them there.

C. (0 pts.) In some instances, finding POC may present a challenge. However, aggressive, creative, and committed organizations are able to locate, recruit, and retain talented POC. Simply concluding that "there are not enough talented POC available" often excuses and encourages managers to settle for poor diversity recruiting results. Offering undeserved praise sends the message that any "effort," even a half-hearted one, counts and that "results" do not. Giving undeserved praise will not lead to the desired change in your managers' performance.

5. You read about the whopping settlements from discrimination charges. Your company may be at risk too! You should:

    0   A. Decide to hire fewer POC to lessen the chances you will be sued too.
    2   B. Talk to companies that have been sued to learn from their mistakes.
    3   C. Call a staff meeting to discuss areas in which your company needs to improve. Then develop and implement a plan to reach improvement goals.
    1   D. Communicate to the employees how these settlements hurt the companies' bottom line.

C. (3 pts.) "C" represents our best choice. Examining your company's weaknesses shows that you are willing to discover where the company is at risk—an important first step to leading change. By involving the staff, you are inviting them to join forces and act as a team to address an issue that impacts everyone. Choosing "C" also shows that you recognize the importance of getting the whole picture in order to resolve difficult situations.

B. (2 pts.) Learning from other companies that have been sued is smart. Yet, the first challenge will be to make sure you understand your own company's issues so you can appropriately apply the lessons learned from others in your organization.

D. (1 pt.) Communicating how the settlements hurt the companies' bottom line is important since maximizing profit is any organization's goal. However, a sole focus on settlement costs will lead you to overlook why the settlements were awarded in the first place.

A. (0 pts.) Hiring fewer POC to lessen the chances you will be sued is shortsighted and ignores a future reality. Demographic trends show a growing number of POC entering the workforce and the dramatic increase in the buying power of POC. You may be placing your organization at a competitive disadvantage by hiring fewer POC.

6. One of the people who reports to you tells you that she does not think all the company's focus on retaining POC is necessary. She says, "Anyone who has ambition can pull himself up by his bootstraps like I did." You should:

    0 A. Tell her to go to a cultural event with POC to gain insights into other cultures.

    2 B. Send her a memo indicating that she is being required to attend the next diversity training session.

    3 C. Challenge her to consider the possibility that "ambition" might not be the only factor that impacts POCs' job satisfaction and retention.

1   D.   Accept that you cannot control the way she feels. As long as she treats everyone the same, her actions are okay.

C.   (3 pts.) While this individual is sharing an opinion that may be considered negative, the good news is that this person is actually having this conversation with you directly. Take this opportunity to ask her why she feels this way and how this view might impact her ability to work effectively with POC. Remind her (1) that success in the organization is not based solely on individual ambition and (2) that other factors such as organizational support, peer support, coaching, mentoring, visibility, and key assign-ments—many of which may have been extended to her—are just as important.

B.   (2 pts.) While attending a diversity class may be a worth-while and necessary experience for this individual, it is likely that she will be angry and resentful about a memo directing her to attend diversity training. After all, she has been very direct with you and probably would have expected the courtesy of having a personal and direct response from you. This indirect method may also lower the chances that she will be candid with you in the future. If the communication channel is shut off, there will be little opportunity for coaching and guidance. Another point to emphasize here is that diversity training should not be used as a solution to address specific diversity issues. These issues are handled most effectively when they are addressed directly with the appropriate individuals.

D.   (1 pt.) It is true that you cannot control the way she feels; however, by ignoring her feelings, you may be missing a key insight, since these feelings determine the way she behaves. Use this opportunity to obtain information about issues that may need to be addressed.

A. (0 pts.) While attending cultural events can be helpful, we should not rely on them as our sole source of diversity education. Attending a religious service, going to a festival, attending a concert, or dining at an ethnic restaurant does not ensure that the person attending will walk away understanding, embracing, or valuing another culture. Unless the individual is committed to learning about diversity, these events are simply experiences that can be enjoyed or dismissed, the same as any other event.

7. A POC who reports to you tells you that he gives 120 percent and that he is not interested in learning to play golf or tennis in order to get ahead. You should:

2 A. Tell him you can appreciate his feeling this way, but explain how and why he may be limiting his opportunities by not participating in these particular sports.

1 B. Ask him if it would be helpful to invite some other POC to come along.

0 C. Tell him to get over it because it's not about fun— it's about succeeding. Then tell him that you pretend to enjoy many things that aren't fun for you.

3 D. Acknowledge that he does give 120 percent. Impress on him the need to develop a broader network and help him brainstorm other ways to expand his network.

D. (3 pts.) It is very important to acknowledge this person's contributions and to emphasize his willingness to give beyond 100 percent. It is also important to respect how he feels about the expectation that he play golf or tennis in order to achieve success. Let him know you want to see him succeed, and tell him you believe in his ability to do so. Take this opportunity to have a candid conversation about other matters, aside from job performance, that are required in order to succeed in the organization. Developing supportive networks, getting exposure, building alliances with individuals outside of his immediate area, and cultivating a positive image may be some examples. Help him identify ways other than participating in sports events to develop networks.

A. (2 pts.) The good news is that you are explaining why extracurricular activities are great opportunities to build relationships that enhance organizational success. However, you are not acknowledging that this employee has a different point of view. He has just told you that he does not want to engage in golf or tennis and that his work contributions are enough. Until you acknowledge his point of view and his feelings, it is unlikely that he will be able to hear or accept your suggestion that this will be good for him.

B. (1 pt.) This response receives only one point because it reflects that, while you are attempting to be responsive to his feelings, you have ignored his point of view. He has not said he was uncomfortable with the setting, nor has he suggested that having other POC present would make him more comfortable. He said he did not want to play tennis or golf in order to get ahead. There may be many other issues at play here. For example, balancing time with family or having the physical ability to play these sports may be issues.

C. (0 pts.) If telling someone to "get over it" would work, most psychologists, psychiatrists, best friends, parents, talk show hosts, *and* managers would be out of business tomorrow. Unfortunately, our feelings, opinions, and beliefs are deep-seated and difficult to change. Telling your employee to "get over it" will most likely lead to resentment and resistance in the future. It is important to understand why he is resisting golf and tennis. Instead of telling him to "get over it," discuss his reluctance. Also provide career guidance to help him see the advantages and disadvantages of his decision.

8. In a training program, a POC openly confronts you about your poor record of developing POC. You should:

0   A. Defend yourself by naming all POC you know and with whom you are friendly.

3   B. Admit that you need to improve your record. Tell the person you plan to learn as much as possible from the training session and invite him or her to continue giving you feedback.

1   C. Share an article that spells out why POC leave organizations, which, by the way, are reasons you cannot control.

2   D. Remind the person that this training program is not supposed to be confrontational. Additionally, let him or her know that he or she has made you uncomfortable. Invite the person to discuss this matter with you privately after the class.

B. (3 pts.) Perhaps the person is telling the truth and there are areas that you need to strengthen. We must be willing to look at ourselves and attempt to view ourselves as others view us. When someone attacks us publicly, one frequent reaction is to attack back. However, it is important to understand our own triggers and hot buttons and to keep negative emotions under control in order to hear what the other person is saying. Even if the person is out of line, retaliation will most likely lead to the situation spinning out of control. Share that you intend to use the session to gain additional insights about your challenges around diversity and that you would welcome the opportunity to speak with that person further and get his or her insights after the session. Reinforce that, while you have personal weaknesses, you are committed to valuing diversity and learning how to manage it effectively.

D. (2 pts.) While you have taken a positive approach in inviting the person to meet with you to discuss the matter privately after class, he or she may only hear your opening statements. By telling the person that his or her behavior in the class is inappropriate and by assuming the role of the victim, you may have reduced the chances that the person will meet you later. It is more important to take advantage of the one-on-one opportunity to meet with this person to hear candid feedback and to determine the merits of the claims than it is to launch a counteroffensive.

C. (1 pt.) Sharing an article about why POC leave organizations ignores the reality of what is occurring in YOUR organization. Additionally, it sends the message that you are avoiding all personal responsibility for what happens to POC in your area. The person has made a direct statement to you. If you respond by sharing a magazine article about an unrelated workplace, you will probably be seen as ignoring a valid concern.

A. (0 pts.) "And your point is?" In this case, "A" is a purely defensive response. Nonetheless, it is a frequent response to diversity challenges. Your acquaintances and friendships outside the workplace have not been called into question. There is no indication that the person is interested in receiving a list of your friends and acquaintances. A more helpful response would be to determine whether, in fact, your record of developing POC is less than stellar. Be open to examining the real image you are projecting, and view your results from an outsider's perspective. Then take steps to make positive changes.

9. One of your best-performing POC tells you she is thinking of leaving. You should:

   1 A. Beg her to stay and offer her a raise.

   2 B. Confide in her that she is on the "high potential" list and that her opportunities will be many if she'll just be patient.

   3 C. Ask her about her experiences at the company and why she is thinking of leaving.

   0 D. Offer to pay for her tuition to attend an MBA school or executive program that requires her to stay with the company for three years after graduation.

C. (3 pts.) Losing any high performer would be a loss to your department. Therefore, treat this person as you would any high-performing employee in your area. Your objective should be to find out what is prompting this statement and to remedy the situation. Be direct and ask her about her experiences with the company and why she is thinking of leaving. If she gives you politically correct responses, be prepared to probe further, albeit respectfully, in order to get to the root cause. After gathering this information, take the necessary steps to address the person's concerns.

B. (2 pts.) This is a scenario that is played out often in corporate America. POC often share that the first time they hear anything about being considered "high potential," having a developmental plan, or being valued by the company is when they announce their intent to leave. The positive is that the information is finally being shared, but it is often too little, too late. Although the company is attempting to meet this person's needs, the person of color is likely to be suspicious and doubt the truthfulness of this feedback because of your timing. A question that is frequently asked by POC in similar situations is, "If I'm so valuable, why haven't I been told before now?"

A. (1 pt.) This response, without other meaningful actions, is often viewed as a knee-jerk reaction. The person has rung the warning bell that something is wrong by telling you that she is THINKING of leaving. The person did not say that she IS leaving! This is an open invitation to find out what is really bothering this person. Often when the response is to simply "throw money" at the person, it is viewed negatively. While the money may be appreciated, it does not resolve organizational culture challenges, interpersonal relationship challenges, support and mentoring challenges, or issues of unequal treatment. In order to meet the long-term needs of this individual, probe for the issues behind the warning bell and find out what can be done realistically to address the situation.

D. (0 pts.) This solution represents a total disconnect (a broken mirror). The individual has alerted you to the possibility of her leaving the organization. You have decided to counteroffer by asking her to commit to another three years at the company, in exchange for a perk she has not requested. There is no attempt to find out what the person really needs in order to remain in the organization. It is possible that you are responding from your perspective of what would make YOU reconsider such a decision. The goal is to understand this POC's perspective.

10. POC have called the diversity initiative a joke. You should:

    2 A. Develop a diversity checklist to track how much progress you are making.

    3 B. Identify specific examples that led them to believe that diversity is a "joke." Address the most critical issues immediately.

    0 C. Host a cultural festival and encourage employees to bring ethnic foods and wear ethnic clothing to demonstrate that diversity is important. This will promote goodwill.

    1 D. Send a memo to everyone in the company. The memo should highlight the progress the company has made in its diversity efforts, including positive comments from two or three POC.

  B. (3 pts.) Do not simply accept the charges blindly, but do not automatically deny them. First, examine whether there is TRUTH in this charge. Tell them that you are interested in learning more and that you will need specific examples to help you understand why they think this initiative is a joke. As the examples are cited, acknowledge those examples that are true and provide insights where information is missing or inaccurate. To demonstrate good faith, identify situations that are critical to be addressed and situations that can be corrected quickly. Share with POC your plan for resolving the remaining issues and follow through on your commitments. Caution! Remember not to take their statement as a personal attack.

A. (2 pts.) While creating a checklist demonstrates good faith in following through on diversity initiatives and sends the message that you are attempting to be responsive, you have not addressed the issue. *POC think the initiative is a joke.* Developing a checklist may do nothing to change a person of color's mind if, for example, he or she thinks the items on the checklist are irrelevant or that no one pays any attention to the items on the list. If either of these is the case, creating a diversity checklist will not address the issue that is troubling to these individuals. Your challenge will be to find the real issue. A question that might help is, "What specifically has happened to convince you that the diversity initiative is a joke?"

D. (1 pt.) After highlighting the progress that the company has made, it is possible that the people in question will respond with a "So what?" The progress of the company, while commendable, may not address the overall diversity needs of the organization. Further, your memo may be interpreted as evading the issue since you have chosen to list accomplishments instead of probing to find out what is really going on in the organization. Many companies are recipients of diversity rewards, are named as one of the best places for POC to work, and receive accolades on innovative diversity processes. Yet in focus groups, POC in some of these same companies often comment, "When we heard about the award, we wondered to which company they were referring!" This scenario demonstrates that

organizational accolades and accomplishments do not
always reflect individual realities.

A. (0 pts.) Festivals are a popular diversity activity. They are
what we refer to as "enhancement" events that can be
effective *supplements* to other diversity efforts. However,
they should not be relied on as the primary way to foster
greater cooperation and team building among diverse
groups. These events tend to be fun, interactive, and infor-
mational. The participants enjoy a wonderful event, and in
most cases they return to their jobs for business as usual.

INTERPRETING YOUR SCORE

0-10	You Have Broken the Mirror! How Many Years of Organizational Bad Luck?
11-20	You Are Picking Up the Pieces
21-29	You Are Putting the Pieces Together Again
30	You Look Mahhhvelous!

In this chapter you have examined how managers' and leaders' decisions can contribute to retention or attrition among people of color. Although these scenarios represent only a small sample of the many types of opportunities that managers and leaders have to discourage or promote retention, they make a point that is central to managing people of color. Managers and leaders must be aware of organizational dynamics that impact people of color, practical in their approach, and skillful in managing their interactions. The next chapter offers specific retention tools that will help you in this pursuit.

CHAPTER 6

Ways to Polish Your Image

Retention Tools

DID YOU LIKE WHAT YOU SAW? Depending on how you assessed your individual behaviors in Chapter 4, how you scored on the Upon Reflection Questionnaire, and your goals for improvement, you may want to develop a plan of action to improve your interactions with POC. The purpose of this chapter is to help you develop that plan. In the next few pages you will find retention tools that will aid you in:

1. Understanding your role in creating an environment that values all employees without regard to differences;

2. Understanding how others perceive you in that role; and

3. Demonstrating "value" for POC and improving retention rates.

Many of the tools that are presented here may stimulate your interest. However, we recommend that you select the ones that are *most* likely to benefit you in achieving the three goals listed above. Choose tools that will help you to develop a concrete plan, and then work your plan.

TOOLS YOU CAN USE

The retention tools are presented in three major sections:

1. *Your Personal View.* This section includes suggestions for analyzing: (a) your thoughts and feelings about managing people from different backgrounds and (b) how those thoughts and feelings impact your decisions and effectiveness. We propose that you use *all* of the tools in this section.

2. *What Others See in You.* This section presents tools to use for obtaining feedback about your effectiveness in managing POC. Select the suggestions that will best address your developmental needs.

3. *Cultivating an Image by Behaving Intentionally and Purposefully.* The tools in this section will help you develop meaningful and sustainable practices that promote retention. As you read through these ideas, identify and act on the ones that will have the greatest impact on your own situation.

Look more closely at yourself.

1. Your Personal View

Personal assessments are often difficult because, in addition to revealing our truly admirable traits, they also expose the less attractive traits that we consciously or unconsciously seek to conceal—even from ourselves. Letting go of virtuous images of ourselves (and our rationalizations for our negative behaviors) is difficult. Even so, looking critically at oneself is a fundamental part of personal development. Whether prompted by others or by some inner desire, taking an *honest* look at oneself is the beginning of personal and professional growth.

When we look beyond surface behaviors to the deeper thoughts and feelings that prompt them, we gain the greatest insights. The tools in this section will prompt you to think at this deeper level. Therefore, we recommend that you use both of the tools in this section, Acknowledge Personal Responsibility and Conduct a Reality Check.

ACKNOWLEDGE PERSONAL RESPONSIBILITY

☀ Acknowledge that you are 100 percent responsible for your beliefs, whether you decide to change them or not.

☀ Think through how you feel by responding to the following questions:

> This process of evaluating my thoughts, feelings, and behaviors about POC makes me feel. . . .
> The idea of having others give me feedback about my interactions with POC is. . . .

☀ Write "I statements" that help you sort through your true feelings about the stereotypes, beliefs, and assumptions you hold about POC.

> , When I interact with people of color:
> I behave like. . . .
> I feel. . . .

As a result, I. . . .

☀ When you are challenged by someone to confront your biases and prejudices, try not to become defensive. Take the responsibility for gathering more information so you can understand why others may view you as biased. Have others clarify by asking:

- What specifically have you observed about my behavior that indicates bias on my part?
- If you were in my shoes, what would you have done differently?

☀ Listen to the responses you receive and examine the merit of their statements.

☀ Since you know best what motivates you, create your own list of ways that you can develop a different perspective.

CONDUCT A REALITY CHECK

☀ Analyze and address your track record.

☀ Overall, how have POC who work for you fared?

☀ Has the record of success for these POC been the same as, better than, or less than that of other employees in your span of control?

☀ Do the employees with whom you have spent the larger portion of your time include POC?

☀ Do the employees you most often assign high-profile or stretch assignments include POC?

☀ Ask yourself, "What would happen if I were convinced that my non-productive beliefs about POC were not true? What would I do differently?"

☀ Complete a diversity assessment to gain an objective understanding of where you stand on diversity criteria such as knowledge of, understanding of, acceptance of, and behavior toward individuals who are different from you. (The Discovering Diversity Profile, a personal assessment tool from Inscape Publishing, is one example of an assessment tool that will give you insight about yourself.)

☀ Continually conduct personal check-ups to assess your beliefs. Ask yourself whether these beliefs are promoting or undermining the results you desire. This is an ongoing, lifelong process. Make it a part of your daily experience.

☀ A powerful check-up question is, "Are my thoughts and behaviors promoting or detracting from my ability to effectively attract, hire, work with, develop, and retain the best talents—irrespective of diversity?"

Look at yourself from another angle.

2. What Others See in You

We don't always project the image that we think we project. Whether we are in leadership roles or not, we often misjudge how we come across to others. As a manager or leader, it is particularly important that you understand how others perceive you. The impressions that you make can significantly impact your relations with POC; and knowing how you are perceived is central to building and sustaining good relationships with employees and promoting retention.

In this section we list tools for determining whether others see you as a barrier or as a catalyst for retaining people of color in your organization.

Seek Feedback

Set the stage before you ask others for feedback. Equip those from whom you are asking for help by doing two things:

1. *Inform Them.* Don't leave people wondering why you want their input. Tell them why and what you hope to accomplish.

2. *Empower Them.* Be certain they are not concerned that you will retaliate or become offended by their input. Ask for and be prepared to receive candid responses. If you have not previously received feedback well, admit this to those from whom you are asking for help. Reassure them that their input will be graciously received.

Next, reference any individual behaviors that you may have highlighted in Chapter 4 for personal development. Determine which of these behaviors you would like to receive feedback on. Consider that some items may be appropriate to share with mentors, coaches, and supervisors and others may be more appropriate to share with employees. When you have set the stage, proceed with the following suggestions:

❉ Develop a simple feedback survey to administer to all individuals in your group on a quarterly basis. Include questions such as:

- Do you feel that you are given the support that you need to succeed in this work group?
- Do you feel that you are appropriately challenged?
- On a scale of 1 to 5, with 5 being the most positive, how would you rate our teamwork and team cooperation?
- What do you need in order to be more successful?
- While there may be issues across the entire team, the goal is to determine whether there are patterns among the responses. Do POC tend to respond differently from the remainder of the team on any given question?

❉ Conduct follow-up discussions with individuals who have presented new insights and suggestions for improvement. Ask open-ended questions (questions that require them to elaborate rather than questions that can be answered in one or two words). If some issues are not clear, ask people to provide examples that will help you to better understand.

❉ Listen carefully and summarize the content and feelings that you hear. Remember to resist the temptation to rationalize and make excuses.

❉ Thank them for their input and tell them what you intend to do next.

❉ Employ 360-degree feedback. Administer a 360-degree feedback instrument and review the feedback to understand how others perceive your actions. Look for indications of perceived bias or prejudice. Be sure several POC are included among your panel of evaluators. Be careful not to select people to participate in your 360-degree evaluation whom you believe are predisposed to be sympathetic to you and your views. In other words, do not stack the deck. You may get results that will make YOU feel comfortable, but these results may not be realistic. (See *Maximizing the Value of 360-Degree Feedback: A Process for Successful Individual and Organizational Development* by Walter Tornow and Manual London.)

❊ Obtain input from a trusted friend who is your regular sounding board and who values diversity. Ask this friend to share his or her observations about your behavior and how you make decisions. For example, ask, "In your opinion, what subtle behaviors contribute to turnover among people of color in my group?" Repeat the request for feedback if he or she hesitates to respond. Follow up with a more personal question: "In your observation, do I demonstrate any behavior that contributes to turnover in my interactions with employees? In my decision making?"

❊ If you have peers who are POC, ask them for feedback in terms of the way in which you relate to POC in general. Ask how they perceive your comfort level around POC, the appropriateness of your behavior, your knowledge of cultures beyond your own, and your natural response to situations that POC face. Be sincere in requesting the feedback, and be non-defensive in receiving it.

❊ Seek feedback from POC outside your immediate environment. Contact POC in other departments, other companies, the community, and other organizations in which you serve to hear their feedback on your interactions and behaviors. (Remember that you will need to provide your reasons for asking for their input. Otherwise, you may not obtain a candid response.)

❊ Ask for candid feedback on your beliefs about and interactions with POC from those who most likely know you best: your spouse, your children, siblings, long-time associates, and parents. Ask: "Based on your observations of me, what do you think are my fundamental beliefs about people of color? What examples of my behavior have led you to think this? Are there specific things that you would suggest that would help me to become more effective in my interactions with people of color?

※ Seek a personal mentor or coach to give you input on your performance managing POC. Share with him or her individual behaviors that you want to improve and check whether they agree that those are behaviors that you need to address. Express your need to receive feedback on issues on which you have insufficient expertise and comfort.

※ Identify a person of color who is at a lower level than you to provide you "reverse mentoring." This process of pairing managers with persons at lower levels of the organization can provide significant insights as long as a level of mutual trust is established at the outset and continues throughout the relationship.

※ Ask colleagues, partners in community work, teammates, and others to share diversity-related experiences they have had with you. Ask them whether they viewed your behavior in each situation as positive or negative.

If you want to look different, behave differently.

3. Cultivating a Different Image by Behaving Purposefully and Intentionally

You have taken two major steps in cultivating a different image—looking more closely at yourself and seeking feedback to determine how others see you. This is where many stop. They become overwhelmed, discouraged, or just dismissive about the information they are given and lose sight of their purpose. Rather than act on the significant insight they have received, they sit on it. As we have seen, this only makes matters worse.

Cultivating a different image will require that you be purposeful (focused) and intentional (action-oriented). Don't drop the mirror now. Reflect on the things that you learned from your self-assessment (Your Personal View) as well as the things that you learned from others (What Others See in You) and prepare to take action.

This section, like the previous ones, includes various ideas that you may wish to incorporate into your plan. However, the most effective actions are thoughtfully planned and executed. So be *purposeful* in deciding what you will do. Remember that your purpose is to *demonstrate "value" for POC and improve retention rates.* Rather than taking actions that only you perceive as helpful, be sure to integrate the recommendations you've received that are most likely to have meaningful and lasting impact. Also remember the significance of being *intentional*: any trust that accrued during the assessment process will be lost unless concrete and meaningful actions follow. Be certain to act on the things that you plan to do.

Carefully review the tools in the sections below and select the ones that will best help you to do the following:

- ❃ Broaden your views;
- ❃ Review and address negative situations;
- ❃ Own and address old behaviors;
- ❃ Understand the new rules of engagement;

* Cultivate diversity-sensitive management skills;

* Be proactive;

* Reward and promote without regard to race; and

* Enhance your image

Broadening Your Views

Whenever you notice that your convictions are hard and fast, revisit them and explore the possibility that your way may not be the only way or the best way. Avoid such narrow views as:

* Discounting the education and technical skills of people of color that were earned from schools that are not on your organization's targeted recruiting list;

* Assuming majority cultural norms, such as a firm handshake or a quick decision, are the real predictors of effective leadership.

Avoid reinforcing negative beliefs about others. Look for indicators that your views may be based on stereotypes rather than reality. (We usually find truth when we earnestly seek it.)

Learn more about individuals from other cultures. Research and read books that expand your insights about different cultures. For example, read *Voices of Diversity,* a book by Renee Blank and Sandra Slipp, or select from the works published by Intercultural Press, Inc. These books, among many others, examine what people have to say about problems and solutions in a workplace where everyone is not alike.

Participate in activities that expand your insights about other cultures, such as book clubs, discussion groups, forums, and panels.

Be an interactive and engaged learner in cross-cultural and diversity training sessions.

Reviewing and Addressing Negative Situations

If you find through your assessment(s) that you have negative beliefs about POC, find out what you need to do differently in order to develop a broader perspective.

If there are situations or scenarios that have resulted in negative feelings between you and a person of color on your team or between a person of color and other team members, invite the person of color to have a confidential conversation with you. Discuss her or his perspectives on the situation, what could have been done to handle the situation more productively, and what should be done at this juncture to get the situation back to normal.

- ☀ Ask for that person's permission to reassess the situation, making no promises other than that you will give it thorough consideration.

- ☀ Evaluate the situation from all angles and determine what you can do as a leader that will be fair, productive, and empowering to the overall team.

❋ If you determine that there are issues that you did not consider previously or that you did not handle the situation appropriately, be willing to admit your error and make corrections.

Focus on (rather than ignore) undercurrents, disputes, and battle-lines that exist in your department. Although they should be addressed under any circumstance, pay special attention to whether these situations exist primarily between individuals who have different diversity characteristics. In other words, assess whether a person of color is involved in a large percentage of these situations.

Owning and Addressing Old Behaviors

Determine whether POC are where they need to be developmentally. Prepare a summary of your evaluation and share this summary with each POC on an individual basis. Ask each person about his or her career goals. Based on the person's responses, initiate the following steps:

❋ Express your willingness to assist the person in his or her development in the future. Be genuine and sincere.

❋ Express your desire to get to know the person better in order to assist in addressing his or her development, goals and aspirations, needs, frustrations, and challenges.

❋ Be clear why you are making this offer at this time, as your new-found interest may be regarded with skepticism.

❋ Be consistent in offering this enhanced level of support in the future.

Understanding the New Rules of Engagement

Spend time with and get to know each person on your team well, especially POC.

❋ Take the initiative to probe and discover all their skills and qualifications.

※ Devote one day per week to having lunch with one of your employees. It may be as simple as a brown-bag lunch.

※ Rotate so that all employees have this opportunity.

※ Develop a routine of dropping by the work areas of at least two of your employees each week for a fifteen- or twenty-minute discussion of their assignments, progress, opportunities, and extracurricular activities.

Be deliberate, creative, and innovative about finding ways (beyond those normally used by others in the organization) to develop people of color. For example:

※ If you are involved in community projects, invite one or two of your employees to work with you on each project. Do not shift the assignment to the employee, but work with him or her as an opportunity to more closely observe the person's work style. Provide feedback, and coach him or her on leadership skills.

※ If you participate in extracurricular activities on behalf of the company, invite a person of color to join you, ensuring that you rotate the opportunity. Be sure to stress that participation is optional and that, if a particular activity is not to his or her liking, the person will have the opportunity to participate in other functions. This can be a great way to develop mutual comfort with POC.

※ Rotate inviting your employees, including POC, to a meeting in which they would not ordinarily participate in order to enhance their exposure and experience.

※ Rotate assignments among your group to allow all team members a variety of experiences and developmental opportunities. Find out what is needed by each to be successful in the respective roles, and work to provide it.

Acknowledge everyone's contributions as well as their developmental needs. Cultivate and manage authentic working relationships with all employees. Look for common values and interests you share with others who are different. Use these common values and interests as a platform to launch meaningful cross-cultural relationships.

Here are some questions that you may use when you talk with POC to get started in the right direction:

1. What specifically would you like me to do to support you in this organization?
2. What types of experiences make you feel uncomfortable in this environment?
3. What types of things are most important for me to communicate to you face-to-face?
4. Do you believe your current role is career-enhancing (providing you with the experiences and skills to ensure your upward mobility)?
5. In what ways are your skills and experiences not effectively utilized in this organization?
6. What changes must occur in order for you to recommend this workplace to other talented POC?
7. To what positions in this organization do you aspire? What is your personal timetable?
8. In your view, what are the chances that you will be able to achieve these aspirations here?
9. Specifically, how do you measure your success as you move toward your ultimate career position?
10. What learning signs will alert me to the fact that you are unhappy here? (What are you likely to do differently?)
11. In what ways will you communicate your concerns to me in the future?
12. What two suggestions would you recommend that I consider in order to support, develop, and accelerate your career?

Cultivating Diversity-Sensitive Management Skills

Talk with all POC in your span of control to encourage them to find mentors. Discuss the value of having a number of mentors, including mentors who will provide cultural comfort, career insight and guidance, feedback on managing their image in the organization, counseling in managing conflict and difficult situations, and developmental experiences. Impress on POC that not all mentors can help them in all of these areas. The goal is to seek a combination of mentors who can provide the full complement of support needed. Offer to help them in this endeavor.

Develop skill in probing for the "real" issues to ensure that the messages you receive are not simply political responses. Some statements by POC that may suggest diversity concerns and the need for further inquiry include:

- I am not sure about my ability to be successful here.
- I am leaving the organization to start my own business, to continue the family business, or to seek a more nurturing community environment.
- My skills and abilities are not adequately matched with roles in this organization.
- The environment in this organization is not supportive.
- My manager has difficulty relating to me.
- I feel as if I am operating on my own.
- I feel as if I am under a spotlight all the time.
- People are nice, but they are not comfortable around me.

As part of your ongoing dialogue with POC in your group, provide candid feedback regarding their performance, their image, their developmental needs, and their interpersonal skills.

- Be clear about your expectations and the rewards for each level of performance.

※ Balance ongoing dialogue with positive reinforcement, coaching, mentoring, and constructive feedback.

※ If a project is less than acceptable or if a POC is not contributing at the level that you require, be consistent in providing immediate, direct, and honest feedback.

※ Give feedback on a job well done, as you would if the person fell short on any task.

※ Remember that feedback that is constructive (sometimes regarded as negative) may be met with defensiveness and distrust if this is the only context in which you engage in dialogue with the individual.

Develop and manage diverse populations in the following ways:

※ Support POC in achieving their potential based on their unique purpose, professional interests, and developmental needs.

※ Actively coach POC and cultivate their skills through direct and indirect methods (mentoring, coaching, developmental planning, sponsoring their participation in seminars and training.)

※ Make development a two-way process. Learn from those you mentor and coach.

※ Recognize that others (including other managers) are always watching and looking to you for cues. Be a positive model for others.

※ Coach and develop the managers who report to you so they are able to comfortably and competently manage diverse work groups too.

Becoming Proactive

Be an advocate, not a crusader, for fairness. If you receive feedback about a person of color that may be potentially damaging to his or her career, ask the person who provided the feedback for clarification and supporting evidence. Of particular importance, ask for evidence beyond one event that supports the person's conclusion. If you have had a different, positive experience with this person of color, share this information to provide balance.

※ Develop a reputation as an individual who is proactive in developing POC in your organization. If there are POC you observe who could benefit from mentoring advice and support at any level, be willing to provide this support and encourage others around you to do so too.

※ Facilitate a discussion or serve as a moderator or a panelist in a forum that addresses multicultural issues. (Remember the adage, "We learn best that which we must teach.")

※ Develop personal relationships with members of groups about whom you have had biases previously.

※ Attract and hire a diverse workforce. The following actions will help:

- Develop relationships and partnerships with educational, business, and social organizations that can source candidates who have diverse backgrounds and experiences.
- Establish relationships with executives of diverse backgrounds with whom you can network.
- Ask employees to help you source diverse candidates. This method will work if you have demonstrated that you truly value a diverse workforce. In fact, you probably will not need to ask for their help. Informal networks will naturally work on your behalf.

Rewarding and Promoting Without Regard to Differences

✳ Invite people to participate on teams, work on special projects, and participate in leadership groups based on actual performance and ability, without regard to race or other differences.

✳ Reward and promote employees based on performance. Reward managers based on their ability to effectively leverage diversity as a means to achieve business goals.

✳ Operate with integrity and be authentic. Walk your talk. Do not recruit, hire, develop, reward, or promote employees because they are POC. At the same time, do not deny them any of these same experiences because they are POC.

✳ Journal your thoughts and actions, and then review your journal periodically. Note when your perspectives and beliefs begin to change. Give yourself "grace," as mistakes will happen. Ask others to do so as well. Changing behaviors that have taken you a lifetime to develop will take time, focus, and repeated effort to correct.

Enhancing Your Image

Taking the steps recommended in this book will require an investment. Your return on investment will be an enhanced image. As you start to act on these recommendations, you will notice positive outcomes. Others will notice them too. Your next challenge will be to ensure that this improved appearance is more than a fleeting image.

Continue to act on what you have learned. Whether you have selected several or a few actions from this chapter to incorporate into your personal plan, treat this plan as you would any business strategy. To ensure long-term results:

✳ Set dates and times for achieving each action.

❋ Ask someone to hold you accountable for each action.

❋ Incorporate items from this plan into your performance objectives.

❋ Proceed as you would with any accountability—work your plan.

❋ Monitor your plan on a regular basis and update it based on your progress.

❋ Correct your mistakes.

❋ Reward your success!

Finally, remember that valuing is a dynamic and ongoing process. Each day and each interaction will present its own opportunities for reflection and improvement. So be vigilant, and every now and then pause again to take a good long look in the proverbial mirror—reflect on your thoughts and feelings and the perspectives of others. Taking the time to understand diverse perspectives—including your own—and behaving purposefully and intentionally to cultivate diverse relationships will help you sustain an image that promotes trust, high performance, and retention.

CLOSING NOTES FROM THE MIRROR

A FEW POINTS TO REMEMBER

- Assume accountability for your impact on others.
- Recognize the need to probe for organization realities.
- Acknowledge that individual interactions and decisions contribute to creating a culture that either values or devalues diversity.
- Recognize that retention is an integrated process that includes four steps. All of which are important!
- Acknowledge that those who do not feel valued often leave.

Finally,

Remember to give yourself "grace" as mistakes will happen. Ask others to do so as well. Changing behaviors that have taken you a lifetime to develop will take time, focus, and repeated effort to correct. Do not allow yourself or others around you to use past inappropriate behaviors as an excuse to abandon your commitment to valuing all employees.

RETENTION IS A NATURAL OUTCOME

Retention, a natural outcome of all of the steps described in this text, cannot be gained through financial incentives alone—retention bonuses, stock options, expense-paid trips, and other lucrative perks. Unless each of the four retention steps—attracting and hiring, relating to and managing, developing, and rewarding and promoting—is established on a foundation of valuing, failure to retain people of color is inevitable. Turnover is a fact of life in organizations, and majority employees as well as people of color will depart. However, the ratio of majority employees who leave compared to people of color who leave the organization will reach a more acceptable balance if leaders and managers focus on valuing people of color.

About the Authors

Janice Fenn, Senior Director of Global Diversity for Kraft Foods, has over twenty years of human resources and diversity experience. Prior to joining Kraft Foods, she was founder and president of the Professional Resources Organization, Inc., a consulting firm specializing in diversity strategy and diversity training seminars working with clients such as Abbott Laboratories, The American Cancer Society, American Express, The DuPont Company, Johnson Controls, McDonald's Corporation, Microsoft, Northwestern Mutual Life Insurance and Time Warner Cable.

Ms Fenn is an advisory board member for the American Institute for Managing Diversity, a board member of the Capital Area Sports Foundation, a not-for-profit organization that promotes and sponsors athletic programs for institutions of higher learning, a member of Leadership America, and was a member the U.S. delegation to Mexico to discuss women's equity issues related to the North American Agreement on Labor Cooperation. She has been honored for achievement by *Dollars and Sense Magazine*, the UNCF College Fund and the YMCA. Ms. Fenn was awarded a lifetime membership in the NAACP in 2003.

Ms Fenn holds both BS and MS degrees in Biology from Tuskegee University, and an MBA from Purdue University's Krannert School of Business.

Chandra G. Irvin is the founder and Principal of Irvin, Goforth & Irvin, LLC, a consulting firm that specializes in improving relationships and performance in diverse environments. Prior to forming Irvin, Goforth & Irvin, she was director of corporate communications and crisis management in a management consulting firm, helping large companies develop strategies to address diversity and public relations crises.

Mrs. Irvin has over twenty years of experience directing operations, human resources, and organization development functions. Her clients have included non-profits and corporations such as Keebler, Kellogg, Sara Lee, Hallmark, Corning, CIGNA, Rohm and Haas, Vanguard, Future Focus 2020, The Center for Work and the Human Spirit, and The Diversity Channel. She manages and facilitates the Diversity Strategy Consortium— a group of corporations that examines domestic and global diversity issues; seeks out diversity best practices; and develops strategies for advancing diversity leadership, accountability, communications, and performance measurements.

Mrs. Irvin earned a M.Ed. degree from the University of South Carolina, a B.S. degree in Business from Winthrop University, completed post-graduate studies at the University of North Texas, and earned professional certifications from national and international management organizations. She is the author of *Finding PEACE in Life, Work, and Love—Listening to the Voice Within.*

INDEX

Pfeiffer Publications Guide

This guide is designed to familiarize you with the various types of Pfeiffer publications. The formats section describes the various types of products that we publish; the methodologies section describes the many different ways that content might be provided within a product. We also provide a list of the topic areas in which we publish.

FORMATS

In addition to its extensive book-publishing program, Pfeiffer offers content in an array of formats, from fieldbooks for the practitioner to complete, ready-to-use training packages that support group learning.

FIELDBOOK Designed to provide information and guidance to practitioners in the midst of action. Most fieldbooks are companions to another, sometimes earlier, work, from which its ideas are derived; the fieldbook makes practical what was theoretical in the original text. Fieldbooks can certainly be read from cover to cover. More likely, though, you'll find yourself bouncing around following a particular theme, or dipping in as the mood, and the situation, dictate.

HANDBOOK A contributed volume of work on a single topic, comprising an eclectic mix of ideas, case studies, and best practices sourced by practitioners and experts in the field.

An editor or team of editors usually is appointed to seek out contributors and to evaluate content for relevance to the topic. Think of a handbook not as a ready-to-eat meal, but as a cookbook of ingredients that enables you to create the most fitting experience for the occasion.

RESOURCE Materials designed to support group learning. They come in many forms: a complete, ready-to-use exercise (such as a game); a comprehensive resource on one topic (such as conflict management) containing a variety of methods and approaches; or a collection of like-minded activities (such as icebreakers) on multiple subjects and situations.

TRAINING PACKAGE An entire, ready-to-use learning program that focuses on a particular topic or skill. All packages comprise a guide for the facilitator/trainer and a workbook for the participants. Some packages are supported with additional media—such as video—or learning aids, instruments, or other devices to help participants understand concepts or practice and develop skills.

- *Facilitator/trainer's guide* Contains an introduction to the program, advice on how to organize and facilitate the learning event, and step-by-step instructor notes. The guide also contains copies of presentation materials—handouts, presentations, and overhead designs, for example—used in the program.

- *Participant's workbook* Contains exercises and reading materials that support the learning goal and serves as a valuable reference and support guide for participants in the weeks and months that follow the learning event. Typically, each participant will require his or her own workbook.

ELECTRONIC CD-ROMs and web-based products transform static Pfeiffer content into dynamic, interactive experiences. Designed to take advantage of the searchability, automation, and ease-of-use that technology provides, our e-products bring convenience and immediate accessibility to your workspace.

METHODOLOGIES

CASE STUDY A presentation, in narrative form, of an actual event that has occurred inside an organization. Case studies are not prescriptive, nor are they used to prove a point; they are designed to develop critical analysis and decision-making skills. A case study has a specific time frame, specifies a sequence of events, is narrative in structure, and contains a plot structure—an issue (what should be/have been done?). Use case studies when the goal is to enable participants to apply previously learned theories to the circumstances in the case, decide what is pertinent, identify the real issues, decide what should have been done, and develop a plan of action.

ENERGIZER A short activity that develops readiness for the next session or learning event. Energizers are most commonly used after a break or lunch to stimulate or refocus the group. Many involve some form of physical activity, so they are a useful way to counter post-lunch lethargy. Other uses include transitioning from one topic to another, where "mental" distancing is important.

EXPERIENTIAL LEARNING ACTIVITY (ELA) A facilitator-led intervention that moves participants through the learning cycle from experience to application (also known as a Structured Experience). ELAs are carefully thought-out designs in which there is a definite learning purpose and intended outcome. Each step—everything that participants do during the activity—facilitates the accomplishment of the stated goal. Each ELA includes complete instructions for facilitating the intervention and a clear statement of goals, suggested group size and timing, materials required, an explanation of the process, and, where appropriate, possible variations to the activity. (For more detail on Experiential Learning Activities, see the Introduction to the *Reference Guide to Handbooks and Annuals,* 1999 edition, Pfeiffer, San Francisco.)

GAME A group activity that has the purpose of fostering team spirit and togetherness in addition to the achievement of a pre-stated goal. Usually contrived—undertaking a desert expedition, for example—this type of learning method offers an engaging means for participants to demonstrate and practice business and interpersonal skills. Games are effective for team building and personal development mainly because the goal is subordinate to the process—the means through which participants reach decisions, collaborate, communicate, and generate trust and understanding. Games often engage teams in "friendly" competition.

ICEBREAKER A (usually) short activity designed to help participants overcome initial anxiety in a training session and/or to acquaint the participants with one another. An icebreaker can be a fun activity or can be tied to specific topics or training goals. While a useful tool in itself, the icebreaker comes into its own in situations where tension or resistance exists within a group.

INSTRUMENT A device used to assess, appraise, evaluate, describe, classify, and summarize various aspects of human behavior. The term used to describe an instrument depends primarily on its format and purpose. These terms include survey, questionnaire, inventory, diagnostic, survey, and poll. Some uses of instruments include providing instrumental feedback to group members, studying here-and-now processes or functioning within a group, manipulating group composition, and evaluating outcomes of training and other interventions.

Instruments are popular in the training and HR field because, in general, more growth can occur if an individual is provided with a method for focusing specifically on his or her own behavior. Instruments also are used to obtain information that will serve as a basis for change and to assist in workforce planning efforts.

Paper-and-pencil tests still dominate the instrument landscape with a typical package comprising a facilitator's guide, which offers advice on administering the instrument and interpreting the collected data, and an initial set of instruments. Additional instruments are available separately. Pfeiffer, though, is investing heavily in e-instruments. Electronic instrumentation provides effortless distribution and, for larger groups particularly, offers advantages over paper-and-pencil tests in the time it takes to analyze data and provide feedback.

LECTURETTE A short talk that provides an explanation of a principle, model, or process that is pertinent to the participants' current learning needs. A lecturette is intended to establish a common language bond between the trainer and the participants by providing a mutual frame of reference. Use a lecturette as an introduction to a group activity or event, as an interjection during an event, or as a handout.

MODEL A graphic depiction of a system or process and the relationship among its elements. Models provide a frame of reference and something more tangible, and more easily remembered, than a verbal explanation. They also give participants something to "go on," enabling them to track their own progress as they experience the dynamics, processes, and relationships being depicted in the model.

ROLE PLAY A technique in which people assume a role in a situation/scenario: a customer service rep in an angry-customer exchange, for example. The way in which the role is approached is then discussed and feedback is offered. The role play is often repeated using a different approach and/or incorporating changes made based on feedback received. In other words, role playing is a spontaneous interaction involving realistic behavior under artificial (and safe) conditions.

SIMULATION A methodology for understanding the interrelationships among components of a system or process. Simulations differ from games in that they test or use a model that depicts or mirrors some aspect of reality in form, if not necessarily in content. Learning occurs by studying the effects of change on one or more factors of the model. Simulations are commonly used to test hypotheses about what happens in a system—often referred to as "what if?" analysis—or to examine best-case/worst-case scenarios.

THEORY A presentation of an idea from a conjectural perspective. Theories are useful because they encourage us to examine behavior and phenomena through a different lens.

TOPICS

The twin goals of providing effective and practical solutions for workforce training and organization development and meeting the educational needs of training and human resource professionals shape Pfeiffer's publishing program. Core topics include the following:

Leadership & Management	Teams & Collaboration
Communication & Presentation	OD & Strategic Planning
Coaching & Mentoring	Human Resources
Training & Development	Consulting
e-Learning	